Sustainability by Design

How One Building in China Could Change the World

Disclaimer

This document was prepared as an account of work sponsored by the United States Government. While this document is believed to contain correct information, neither the United States Government nor any agency thereof, nor The Regents of the University of California, nor any of their employees, makes any warranty, express or implied, or assumes any legal responsibility for the accuracy, completeness, or usefulness of any information, apparatus, product, or process disclosed, or represents that its use would not infringe privately owned rights. Reference herein to any specific commercial product, process, or service by its trade name, trademark, manufacturer, or otherwise, does not necessarily constitute or imply its endorsement, recommendation, or favoring by the United States Government or any agency thereof, or The Regents of the University of California. The views and opinions of authors expressed herein do not necessarily state or reflect those of the United States Government or any agency thereof or The Regents of the University of California.

ISBN-13:978-0692341155 (Sustainable by Design)
ISBN-10:0692341153

Funding Statement

This work was supported by the Southern China Green Office Building Technology Integration and Demonstration Project Group, Shenzhen Institute of Building Research Co., Ltd (IBR), under Fund Code 2012A010800021; and the Assistant Secretary for Energy Efficiency and Renewable Energy, Building Technologies Program of the U.S. Department of Energy under Contract No. DE-AC02-05CH11231.

Photo credits: Shenzhen IBR.

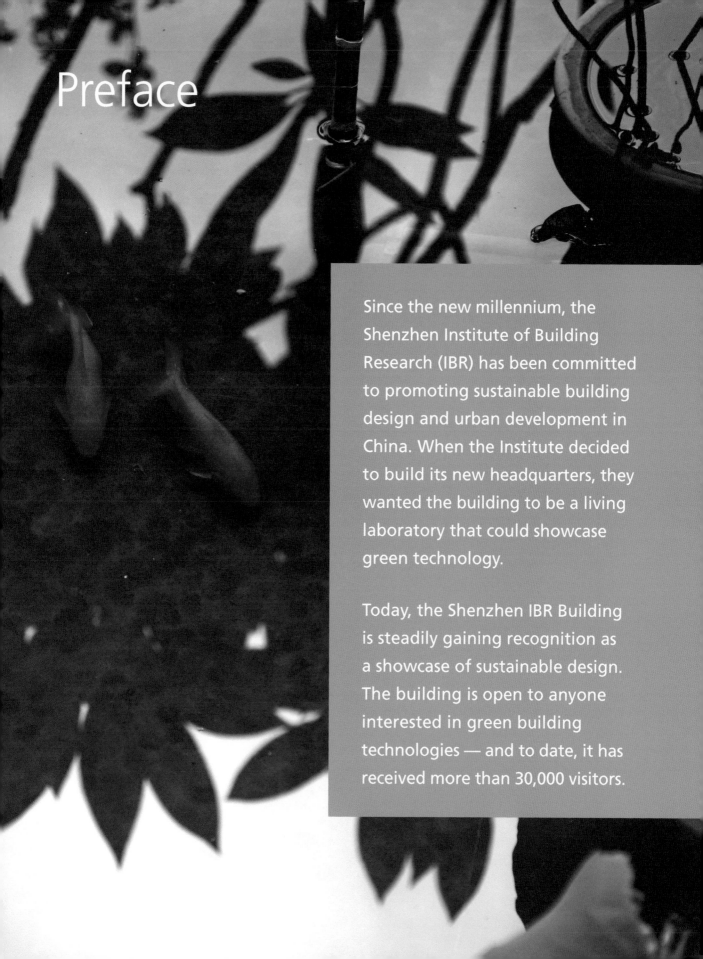

Preface

Since the new millennium, the Shenzhen Institute of Building Research (IBR) has been committed to promoting sustainable building design and urban development in China. When the Institute decided to build its new headquarters, they wanted the building to be a living laboratory that could showcase green technology.

Today, the Shenzhen IBR Building is steadily gaining recognition as a showcase of sustainable design. The building is open to anyone interested in green building technologies — and to date, it has received more than 30,000 visitors.

On closer inspection, this pioneering building reveals an abundance of carefully designed features that are making it a model for green architecture not just in China, but throughout the world as well. These features include:

- More than 40 sustainable technologies that were incorporated into a low-cost, low-energy building through the use of integrated design principles.

- A design focus on daylighting and natural ventilation, which greatly reduced the energy loads for lighting and air conditioning.

- Workspaces designed to emphasize communication and a people-friendly environment. (As a result, workers in the building report high levels of satisfaction with their workspaces.)

- Integrating nature with the workplace to provide an environment that is both stimulating and restorative. Innovations included generously landscaped areas, such as the novel Sky Garden on the sixth floor, and elevations designed to capture the benefits of the wind and sun.

Unlike green showcases that achieved low-energy performance at a high-cost premium, the Shenzhen IBR Building was built at a lower cost than that of new commercial structures in Shenzhen. The architects kept the total per-square-meter construction cost in 2009 to RMB 4300 Yuan/m^2 ($70/ft^2), which is a remarkably low number considering all of the sustainable measures included in the project. Part of the reason for this low cost of construction was that the design team pursued a strategy of integrated design, finding the optimal combination of systems that could reduce construction costs. The IBR managed the entire building's design, construction, and operation stages through this integrated approach.

The Shenzhen IBR Building has recorded remarkably low energy usage. The building's Energy Use Intensity (EUI) for the 12-month period between 2011 and 2012 was 63 kWh/m^2 (20 kBtu/ft^2) is 61% of the mean EUI value of 103 kWh/m^2 (33 kBtu/ft^2) for similar buildings in the region. In addition, the Shenzhen IBR Building requires less than a third of the energy used by U.S. green office buildings whose mean EUI of 66 kBtu/ft^2 is 25% lower than the average for U.S. office buildings.

The Shenzhen IBR Building has achieved low energy use without compromising user satisfaction. According to a recent survey, 94% of indoor personnel said they were satisfied with the IBR Building's overall indoor environment. Specifically, over 80% said they were satisfied with the building room temperature; over 85% said they were satisfied with the indoor sound levels; more than 80% said they were satisfied with the indoor lighting; and 95% expressed satisfaction with the indoor air quality.

In recognition of its high performance with low-energy usage, the IBR Building has received more than 30 awards, including:

- Leadership in Sustainable Design & Performance (World Green Building Council's Asia Pacific Regional Network Leadership Awards in Green Building), 2014
- The German Energy Agency (DENA) Energy Efficiency Award, 2013
- First prize in Building Engineering by the People's Republic of China Ministry of Construction for National Engineering Excellence and Design in 2011
- First Grade (highest score) of the 2010 National Green Building Innovation Award (China)
- First place in the National Demonstration Project of Renewable Energy Application (China), 2010
- First place in the National Top 100 Green Building Demonstration Projects (China), 2010

We see the Shenzhen IBR Building not as a facility to be copied, but as the model for a process that can be replicated. If others can learn how this process was applied to this building, it will make possible many more sustainable design projects in China and elsewhere. As a model of sustainable design, the Shenzhen IBR Building could indeed change the world.

Table of Contents

1. Introduction: A View to the Future

While China's rapid modernization has given birth to a growing middle class, its rising prosperity has come at the expense of its environment and air quality, just as it has for other industrialized nations in the past. In January 2013, thick and severe smog blanketed almost all of China's east coast. In Beijing, air pollution readings during the Chinese New Year were 40 times the World Health Organization's air-quality guidelines.[1] There is perhaps no better demonstration of the urgent need to address China's environmental issues and green the economy. Is China ready and able to do so? We think so, and are encouraged by the nascent green building movement that is developing in China today.

1.1 Goal of This Book

The goal of this book is to present a model for future green development in China, the United States, and the rest of the world. The idea is not that a single building can be replicated, but that the process and spirit that guided the design, construction, and operation of one highly successful building can be studied, absorbed, and spread throughout the global architectural community. Ye Qing, the visionary President and Chairman of the Shenzhen Institute of Building Research (IBR), has said that she wants the world to know how the Chinese design buildings that reflect local technologies and conditions. She wants to share their stories so others can learn from both their mistakes and successes. Her vision is that this green design will set a standard for sustainable building architecture throughout the world.

1.2 The IBR Vision: A Quiet Revolution?

The Shenzhen IBR was founded in 1992 as a comprehensive science and technology research institute focused on building energy efficiency, green building technologies, and low carbon eco-cities. IBR today provides services for the whole life cycle of buildings and urban development. Its specialties include research and consultation, urban and rural planning, sustainable design, project quality inspection, materials and indoor environment testing, project management, and the dissemination of information about building research. In 2008, IBR was accredited as a National High-Tech Enterprise and was recognized as the "Most Influential Organization of Building Energy Efficiency in China." Currently, IBR has a staff of over 400 workers. In 2011, the turnover exceeded 190 million Yuan ($30 million).

IBR's mission statement establishes its dedication to "cutting-edge research with the pursuit of providing technologies and happiness for the masses instead of elites, serving the public instead of the privileged few." As one of the early champions in this field, IBR was famous for its "Shenzhen Model" of development, focusing on both green buildings and green city planning. In recent years, IBR has worked on building projects totaling more than 300 million square meters, and rural and urban planning projects involving over 3,000 square km. Together, these projects have yielded estimated savings of more than 300 million kWh of energy.

IBR is committed to "eternally and ultimately pursuing an advocacy for a kind of green life concept in China, which is a sharing, balanced, lifespan-oriented and human-environmentally harmonized philosophy of view, way of thinking, methodology, and even a lifestyle — that such a 'green' self-conscious person continues not only at work but extends throughout a career, not only for private living, but also for public behavior."

1.3 Who Is This Book For?

We wrote this book for architects, planners, educators, building owners, managers and operators, policy makers, and others who believe that green buildings will help contribute to a sustainable world. Designers and planners will see how an integrated design can lead to low energy performance. Educators can take the design philosophy and extend it to the needs and specific requirements of their students. Building owners and managers can see how the green models used in the Shenzhen IBR Building can be replicated in their buildings, both new and existing. And finally, policy makers can see how requirements, incentives, and recognition for integrated design can develop a culture in which green buildings can flourish.

1.4 Acknowledgments

We offer our deepest thanks to our many friends and colleagues at the Shenzhen IBR who made this work possible. They provided warm hospitality during our visits, answered our numerous questions over the course of writing this book, and shared their extensive data and information about the building. Of the many people at IBR to whom we are indebted, we want to first thank Ye Qing, visionary, architect, and president of the Shenzhen IBR. Her colleagues who helped us in the work include Liu Junyue, Mao Hongwei, Li Yutong, Liu Zongyuan, Lu Zhen, GuoYongcong, Yu Han, and Wu Zhenzhen.

We also want to thank our LBNL colleagues, starting with Dr. Mark Levine, founder of the China Energy Group at Lawrence Berkeley National Laboratory, who made the initial connections with Ye Qing that led to the development of this work. And we would also like to thank LBNL Public Affairs Creative Services for their excellent work on the editing and design for this book. Our China Energy Group colleagues Lynn Price, Nan Zhou, Yao Yuan, and Brian Heimberg all played supporting roles throughout the project, offering thoughtful advice, helpful direction, and good humor whenever needed.

2. Today: Buildings in China

2.1 Current Status of Buildings in China

Commercial buildings are springing up in China at an enormous pace — roughly 500 million square meters per year — five times the annual projected growth for commercial buildings in the U.S. through 2030.

In 2008, the total commercial floor space in the U.S. topped 7.6 billion square meters, slightly more than China's total of roughly 7.1 billion square meters.[2,3]

Downtown Shenzhen 1982.

The Ministry of Housing and Urban & Rural Development (MOHURD) regulates building construction in China. Key responsibilities of MOHURD include development, supervision, and management at the national level of building energy-efficiency policies and projects.

MOHURD's provincial and local branches are responsible for developing, supervising, and managing building energy-efficiency policies and projects within their administrative regions (Figure 1, see page 10). These branches are charged with assisting in the implementation of national building energy-efficiency policies and projects at the provincial, city, and county levels.

Shenzhen today. *Source: © iStock.com*

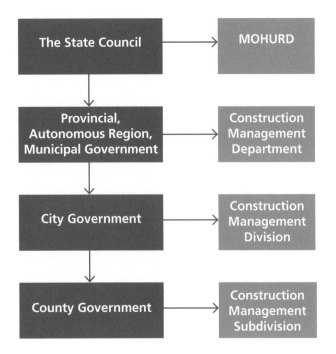

2.2 Impact of Buildings on Climate Change

The buildings sector accounts for nearly one-fifth of total primary energy consumption in China. During a 12-year period, from 1996 to 2008, primary energy consumption by buildings in China grew 1.5-fold, reaching a level equivalent to 687 million tons of coal equivalent (Mtce) of primary commercial energy consumption (or 814 Mtce including bio-energy consumption) by 2011.[4] When we consider that China already accounts for nearly half the world's total coal consumption (Figure 2) the impact of buildings in China on global carbon- dioxide emissions is clearly evident.[3]

Energy intensity in buildings — the amount of energy consumed per unit of floor area — differs significantly across varied climate zones. During the first decade of this century, the Hot Summer Cold Winter (HSCW) zone experienced a significant increase in energy use during the long winter heating period, while in both the HSCW and the Hot Summer Warm Winter (HSWW) zones cooling energy use skyrocketed.[2] Energy intensity in buildings also differs significantly according to the type of structure. For example, electricity intensity in large public buildings (>20,000 square meters) is often two to three times higher than that in smaller public buildings.

Carbon-dioxide emissions associated with building energy use reached approximately 1.98 billion tons in 2012. Experts within and outside China agree that there exists a huge potential for curtailing the increase in energy demand and reducing greenhouse gas (GHG) emissions by improving energy efficiency in China's building sector.[2]

Figure 1. Administrative structure for commercial building construction in China. *Source: Shui 2012*

2.3 Status of Green Buildings in China and the United States

In 2007, MOHURD initiated a program to establish green-building demonstration projects involving buildings in the planning stage, under construction, or completed within the prior year. Applications were considered for commercial buildings larger than 20,000 square meters, and for residential communities or groups of communities larger than 100,000 square meters. Projects were evaluated for green labels either for their design or for their actual operation. During the six years of the program, a total of 1,446 buildings were awarded with green labels (Figure 3, see page 12).

By December 2013, the projects in China that received green building certificates had a total construction floor area of 162.7 million square meters. China has set a target that more than 80% of new, government-funded building construction meet green label standards by the end of the 12th Five-Year Plan (FYP) in 2015, and that a total of one billion square meters of new green building construction be finished during the 12th FYP.

Coal Consumption: China Rivals the Rest of the World

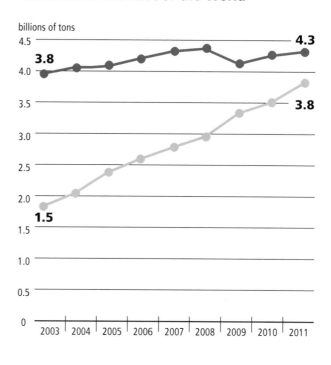

Figure 2. China's coal consumption compared with the rest of the world. *Source: U.S. Energy Information Administration, International Energy Statistics.*

Number of Green Commercial Building Projects in China, 2008 – 2013

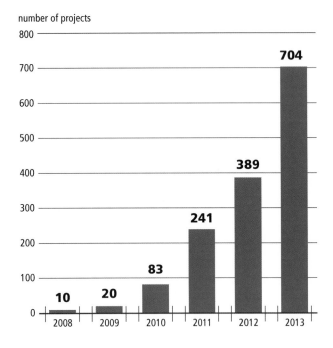

number of projects

2.4 The City of Shenzhen

Shenzhen is a major city in Guangdong Province, situated just north of Hong Kong, in the south central region of China (see Figure 4).

Modern Shenzhen was the first of five Special Economic Zones (SEZs) established by China and remains one of the most successful. It is the product of a strong economy made possible by rapid foreign investment since the institution of the policy of "reform and opening" and the establishment of the SEZ in late 1979. Both Chinese and foreign nationals have invested enormous amounts of money in the Shenzhen SEZ. More than US$30 billion in foreign investment has gone into both foreign-owned and joint ventures. Those investments focused primarily in manufacturing initially, but more recently have expanded to the service sector as well. Shenzhen is now one of the fastest-growing cities in the world.

Figure 3. Number of green commercial building projects in China, 2008–2013. *Source: CSUS 2014*

Source: © iStock.com

Guangzhou

Shenzhen

Hong Kong

Macau

Figure 4. Map showing location of Shenzhen. *Source: Image © 2014 TerraMetrics*

3. Designing the IBR Building

When the Shenzhen IBR design team envisioned their new headquarters, they thought of it as a green experiment.[5] As both architect and client for the project, the design team could expand their green agenda beyond what their counterparts were doing in China and elsewhere. The team reviewed over 100 sustainable technologies and strategies, and incorporated forty of them, including daylighting; natural ventilation; gray-water recycling; solar-energy generation; and highly efficient heating, ventilation, and air-conditioning (HVAC) systems. The 12-story building with 18,000 square meters of floor space was designed during 2006 and 2007. Construction was completed in March 2009.

According to IBR President Ye Qing, the Institute's team implemented the green design principles of "localization, low-energy consumption, and finely detailed design." Ye wanted the IBR headquarters to showcase the best sustainable building practices, while differentiating it from other green buildings in China that were expensive and reliant on new and unproven energy-saving technologies.[5] The designers of the IBR Building set the goal of creating a fully sustainable building, one that would use resources wisely, provide a comfortable work environment, and serve as a model for others interested in designing low-energy buildings.

The green design of IBR focuses on three elements: people, resources, and the environment, as shown in Figure 5. To serve these three core elements, the design was carried out to ensure excellence in meeting six criteria:

- Land savings

- Water savings and the use of natural water resources

- Indoor air quality

- Energy efficiency and renewable energy harvesting

- Materials savings and natural materials utilization

- Operations and management

To meet these goals, the IBR Building design team took into account climate, economy, policies, culture, technology, and management. The next section describes in more detail IBR's design philosophy.

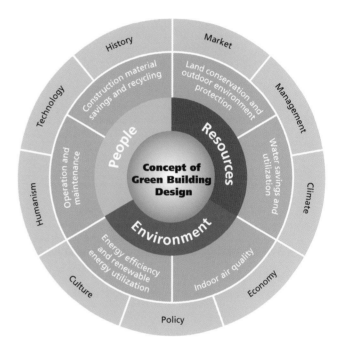

Figure 5. Concept of green building design.

The IBR Building follows the design philosophy known as the "Five Practices."

PRACTICE 1:
Sharing of Design

PRACTICE 2:
Sharing of People and Nature

PRACTICE 3:
Sharing from Person to Person: 1 + 1 = 4

PRACTICE 4:
Sharing of Building & Society: A Building as "Good Citizen"

PRACTICE 5:
Sharing of Daily Life and Daily Work

3.1 The "Five Practices for Green Design"

Practice 1: Sharing of Design. This fundamental principle recognizes that building design is a shared process, one that involves the rights and resources of all the parties, and that everyone has the right to join in the design process. All people affected by the design, construction, and use of a building have the right to express their concerns.

Further, the building itself is literally a platform for sharing, one that provides an efficient and economical basis for interaction among human beings, and between humans and nature. Green building design provides not only a comfortable place for the highly efficient use of resources, but also a platform for human behavior and culture, affecting lifestyles, communication, and thinking.

The basic rule of Sharing of Design is one of balance. The elements that need to be considered in this equation include the whole building life cycle (raw materials acquisition, manufacturing, transportation, installation, use, and waste management) and the physical environment, including the relationship between occupants and the indoor and outdoor environment as well as the relationship between the building and the surrounding areas. The third element is systems integration, which includes technology and market forces as well as weather and culture. The successful integration of a green building requires more than just the assemblage of these diverse parts.

Practice 2: Sharing of People and Nature. The goal of green building design is to create comfortable, resource-sparing, environmentally friendly surroundings. The desire is to find in nature qualities that have been almost completely lost in the industrialized world. Architecture should create comfortable environments that bring humanity and nature together harmoniously, recognizing that human beings and nature share one world.

In practice, this means an IBR Building design that works with four elements: wind, light, land, and water:

1. **Wind:** Using natural ventilation during spring and fall reduces the need for mechanical air conditioning.

2. **Light:** Daylight for all the office spaces means no artificial lighting is needed during the day, while providing views of the surrounding mountains from all the workstations.

3. **Land:** A vertical landscape throughout the building doubles the area available for greenery compared to the building's original footprint. The roof garden, aerial garden, and patio garden all help restore the ecological balance of the building site.

4. **Water:** In 2013, a 43% savings in water consumption, compared to that of similarly sized conventional buildings, was achieved through the use of storm-water collection and reclaimed water.

Practice 3: Sharing from Person-to-Person: 1 + 1 = 4. The challenge of exchanging ideas is a fundamental concern for people in the modern city. As explained by the Shenzhen IBR design team, Sharing from Person-to-Person is a practice where, if you have an idea and I have an idea, and we then exchange those ideas, we would then each have two ideas, for a total of four. With these four ideas we can influence other people. New communication technologies such as email, smartphones, and text messaging improve communication efficiency but may not improve communication quality.

The Shenzhen IBR designers wanted to encourage quality communication and connection among those who work in their new building. Nearly 40% of the floor space is dedicated to direct, person-to-person communication, including areas in the lobby, conference rooms, aerial gardens, the roof garden, multipurpose rooms, open stairwells, and leisure patios at each floor. These and other open spaces are where chance and planned encounters can lead to idea generation and development.

Practice 4: Sharing of Building & Society: A Building as "Good Citizen." Buildings consume significant resources, such as concrete, steel, water, and electricity, and they have major impacts on a city and the surrounding environment. Buildings are also "citizens" of a city and, as such, have obligations to society. Part of a building's obligation as a "citizen" is to give back to the city, whether through open space, or to provide spaces for citizen activities, such as public meetings, exhibitions, and education.

The Shenzhen IBR Building is designed to minimize its footprint, and as already noted, to restore nature through its vertical landscaping. Buses and bicycles have priority for transportation, and the parking places provided are limited. A "visitor's route" for the public was designed to allow visitors to walk through the building and learn about the sustainable features without distracting the workers. Recognizing an "obligation for self-discipline," the design team set targets for energy savings of 60% and water reduction of 40% compared to conventional buildings in the region. To verify this commitment, the building has a detailed monitoring and management system whereby staff can track consumption on an hourly basis.

Practice 5: Sharing of Daily Life and Daily Work.
Work is part of our daily life, and we all need to create the right balance between work and our other pursuits of family life, community, and well-being. The IBR Building is a platform for supporting work and life, and includes several features to promote the well-being of staff such as the vegetable farm, a weekend cinema, coffee rooms, a karaoke room, a gym, a children's playground, an employee poster wall, and a meditation room.

3.2 Working with Nature

China has a diverse set of regional climate zones, ranging from "Severe Cold" in the northern and western plateaus, to the "Hot Summer/Warm Winter" (HSWW) in the south (Figure 6). Shenzhen is located in the HSWW zone, with mean monthly winter temperatures generally above 10°C (50°F) and mean monthly summer temperatures in the range of 18–25°C (64–77°F).

Climate is one of the most important factors in determining the energy use in a commercial building. The IBR design team took into consideration the local climate (see Figure 7) to minimize the amount of energy needed to condition and illuminate the workspaces. Their climate strategies included working with sunlight for passive heating, and shading the envelope to reduce overheating. Photovoltaic materials were often used to take advantage of the incident sunlight.

Climate Zones in China

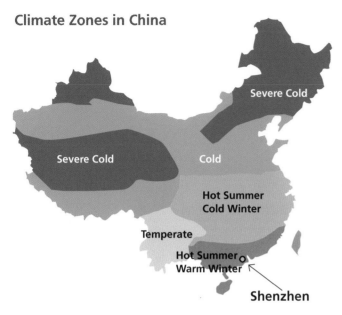

CLIMATE ZONES	MEAN MONTHLY TEMPERATURE	
	COLDEST	HOTTEST
Severe Cold	≤ -10 °C	≤ 25 °C
Cold	-10 – 0 °C	18 – 28 °C
Hot Summer/Cold Winter	0 – 10 °C	25 – 30 °C
Hot Summer/Warm Winter	> 10 °C	25 – 29 °C
Temperate	0 – 13 °F	18 – 25 °C

Figure 6. Climate zones in China. *Source: Huang and Deringer (2007) and MOHURD (1993).*[2]

Climate Data for Shenzhen (1971–2000)

MONTH	JAN	FEB	MAR	APR	MAY	JUN	JUL	AUG	SEP	OCT	NOV	DEC	YEAR
Average high °C (°F)	20 (67)	19 (67)	22 (73)	26 (79)	29 (85)	31 (88)	32 (90)	32 (90)	31 (88)	29 (84)	25 (77)	21 (71)	**27 (80)**
Daily mean °C (°F)	15 (59)	15 (60)	19(66)	22 (72)	26 (78)	28 (82)	29 (83)	28 (83)	27 (81)	25 (76)	20 (69)	16 (61)	**23 (73)**
Average low °C (°F)	12 (53)	13 (55)	16 (61)	20 (68)	23 (74)	2 5(77)	26 (78)	25 (78)	24 (76)	22 (71)	17 (63)	13 (55)	**20 (67)**
Rainfall mm (inches)	30 (1)	44 (2)	67 (3)	17 4(7)	238 (9)	296 (12)	339 (13)	368 (14)	238 (9)	99(4)	37 (1)	34 (1)	**1,966 (77)**
Avg. rainy days (≥ 0.1mm)	7	10	11	13	16	18	17	18	15	8	6	6	**144**
% Humidity	72	77	79	81	82	82	80	82	79	72	68	67	**77**
Mean monthly sunshine hours	148	99	101	110	150	174	220	189	181	199	184	178	**1,934**

Figure 7. Climate data for Shenzhen (1971–2000).

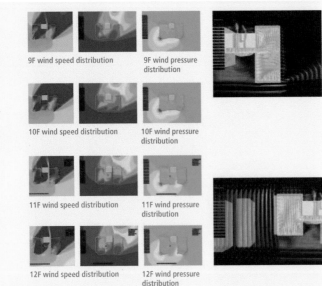

9F wind speed distribution — 9F wind pressure distribution

10F wind speed distribution — 10F wind pressure distribution

11F wind speed distribution — 11F wind pressure distribution

12F wind speed distribution — 12F wind pressure distribution

from top to bottom:
Figure 8. Site plan for the IBR Building.
Figure 9. Wind pressure studies on the site of the IBR Building.
Figure 10. Parking for bike commuters.

3.3 Site Analysis

The IBR Building is located in northern, central Shenzhen, and is close to bus and subway stations. Mountains from the north, west, and east surround the 3,000-square-meter site, which was formerly an abandoned quarry.

The designer used computer simulations of the airflow at the site to predict building performance and provide design feedback. Figure 9 illustrates the wind-pressure field around the IBR Building. This analysis provided important information for zone designs incorporating natural ventilation.

3.4 Green Transportation

Transportation was an important consideration in the site selection and design of the IBR Building. The primary modes of transportation for the staff were intended to be bicycle, bus, and the nearby metro. Bicycle parking spaces were included to encourage employees to choose this greenway to commute (Figure 10). The IBR Building provides shower rooms for bicycle commuters.

3.5 Sustainable Strategies for the IBR Building

The IBR design team started with the passive solar heating and daylighting principles suitable for their hot-summer and warm-winter regional climate. Next, they emphasized the integration of technologies, choosing the best and coordinating these technologies throughout multiple systems. They used their Building Information Models (BIM) system to perform simulations and applications and to determine the most effective strategies. The result was a novel building layout based on systems analyses of structural design and functional zoning. Table 1, below, summarizes the green-technology enhancements the IBR Building design team chose from over a hundred different sustainable technologies and strategies.

Table 1. Sustainable Strategies for the IBR Building

LAND CONSERVATION AND OUTDOOR ENVIRONMENT	**Utilization of Underground Space**	Parking, machine room, & bicycle storage
	Outdoor Protection	The retention and reuse of soil and water
	Special Design	Planting native plants
	Construction Control	Green construction measures
ENERGY SAVING AND ENERGY UTILIZATION	**Renewable Energy Systems**	Passive daylight technology (the basement and indoor natural lighting)
		Natural ventilation control
		Semi-centralized solar water-heating system to provide hot water showers on each floor, and centralized solar water-heating system to provide hot water for guest apartments and the cafeteria
		Solar photovoltaic systems to provide power supply for underground garage, stair rooms, corridors, and other public areas
		Breeze-start wind generators
	Wall system	Window-wall ratio and shape coefficient control
		Exterior insulation
		Light colored surfaces
	Windows and Doors (Glass) System	Insulated and hollow Low-E aluminum alloy doors and windows
	Roofing System	Planted roof
	Sun-shading System	Building unit shading (Photoelectric visors, etc.)
		Exterior shadings (louver dampers, etc.)
	Distribution Lighting System	Energy-saving lamps, fixtures, and controls
	Air-conditioning	Water-loop heat pump, water-source heat pump, temperature, humidity independent control, and other high-efficiency and energy-saving air conditioning
WATER SAVING AND WATER RESOURCE UTILIZATION	**Water-saving Equipment System**	Water-saving appliances, variable velocity/variable frequency technology
	Recycled Water System	Recycled water flushing, waterscape, greening and air conditioning cooling water
		Rainwater recycling
	Landscape Water Quality Conservation	Artificial wetland purification treatment

Continued on next page

Table 1. Sustainable Strategies for the IBR Building *Continued from previous page*

MATERIAL SAVING AND MATERIAL RESOURCE UTILIZATION	**New recycling pipe (copper pipes, polypropylene, polyethylene pipe)**	
	Structure Material (high-strength concrete and high-performance concrete, etc.)	
	Local/Native Material	
	Wood products with more than 10% recycled materials	
	Refuse-classification collection system	
INDOOR ENVIRONMENTAL QUALITY	**Lighting Technology**	Indoor natural lighting design
	Pollutant Control Technology	Anti-condensation, anti-fungal
	Technology	Interior finishes with low emissions
	Noise Control Technology	Doors and windows, floors, separating wall sound insulation
		Pipe acoustic treatment (noise elimination, absorber)
		Equipment acoustic (vibration isolator, floating building floor, sound absorbing material, etc.)
	Air Humidity and Temperature Control Technology	Natural ventilation
		Indoor temperature control
OPERATION MANAGEMENT	**Construction equipment automatic monitoring and energy using classification metering system**	

Green Design Features That Were Considered but Not Included

The design team considered several other green design features that did not make it into the final design. These included adjustable exterior shading technologies and a greater use of recyclable building materials. The primary reason for not pursuing these strategies was their cost.

3.6 **Basic Building Organization**

The architects designed the structure as a set of building blocks. By organizing portions of the building into various blocks and stacking them, the architects were able to create a 12-story outdoor atrium on the east side that captures southeasterly breezes and brings daylight deep inside (Figure 11). Photovoltaic panels covering the atrium provide clean energy — part of China's first state-level renewable energy demonstration project. These three-dimensional stacked functions are a unique aspect of the IBR Building design.

Floor Plan

The floor plan for a typical office space is shown in Figure 12. The white areas are office space and the yellow areas are open corridors. The U-shaped design allows the wind to flow through open corridors of the building and enhances the effects of natural ventilation.

Exterior Envelope

The IBR Building has a thermal envelope that is differentiated on each elevation. The building envelope has Low-E double-paned windows with frames made from an aluminum alloy, providing good daylight, thermal, acoustic, and anti-freezing performance. Based on the IBR specifications, the windows have the following characteristics: effective U-factor for assembly, 3.5~4.0 W/m² K; solar heat gain coefficient (SHGC), 0.35 max; and visual transmittance, 0.45 min.

Figure 11. Organization of the basic building elements for the IBR Building.

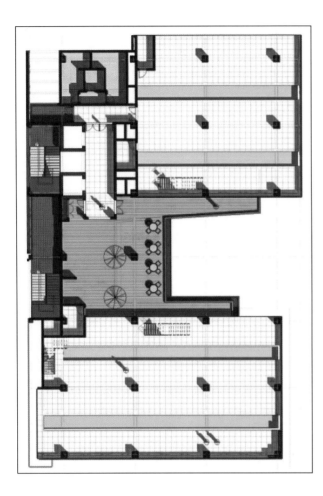

Different window-to-wall ratio (WWR) numbers are used for different areas of the building. The lower areas of the building are designed primarily for labs and conference rooms, where a WWR value of 0.3 was used for the south, east, and north elevations to minimize daylight impact on lab testing and conference space. The upper part of the building is used for office space, where a WWR value of 0.7 was chosen to make use of daylight and reduce energy consumption from artificial lighting.

Shading is important for buildings located in China's Hot Summer Warm Winter (HSWW) climate region, and the IBR Building adopted different shading strategies for different elevations. Overhangs with interior screens are used for office rooms. Vegetation is planted to cover parts of the building's west-side facade. The opaque part of the building envelope consists of insulation materials and aluminum exterior finishing on cast concrete, which makes the building

Figure 12. Floor plan of a typical office floor.

envelope easy to clean and maintains good thermal integrity. The west side of the building facade is integrated with thin-film photovoltaic (PV) panels. This PV-integrated facade has a visible transmittance of 0.2, which maintains acceptable visibility while harvesting renewable energy for building operations.

Figure 13 shows the main entrance and the exterior elevations of the first through fifth floors. The lower floors are exhibition halls and testing labs. Note the large open staircase on the exterior, which encourages walking, rather than elevator use, between floors.

Figure 14 shows an example of the overhang shading that is commonly found on the office floors.

Figure 15 shows the exterior-wall finishing, which is an assembly of aluminum cladding and insulation materials. This assembly is easy to install, provides good thermal insulation, and makes for an energy-efficient building shell.

from top to bottom:
Figure 13. Exterior of first through fifth floors.
Figure 14. Exterior window shading.
Figure 15. Exterior aluminum finishing.

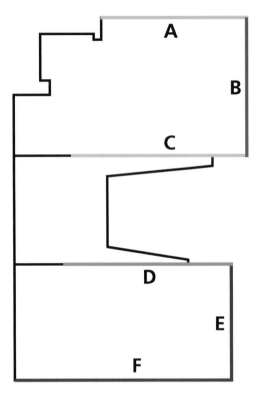

3.7 **Window Design and Orientation**

Different window systems were considered during the IBR Building's design stage. The designers evaluated each type of window's opening system and effective natural ventilation area.

Figure 16 shows the location of different window types for the office floors, each oriented to take advantage of the prevailing wind. The north facade (A) and north-facing elevation (D) use the left-horizontal-open single-hung sash. For the east-facing elevations (B) and (E), the designers selected horizontal pivoting windows to maximize the open area. The south facade (F) and south-facing elevation (C) use the right-horizontal-open single-hung sash.

Table 2 shows the window and facade areas for each elevation of the building, along with the calculated window-to-wall ratio. The IBR Building also uses different window-to-wall ratios in different functional floor spaces. At the first through fifth levels, the window-to-wall ratio is designed to be 30%, reflecting a lesser need for natural lighting in the laboratory areas; while at the seventh through 12th levels (the office floors), a higher window-to-wall ratio of 70% is used. This design makes sure the building can

Figure 16. Typical floor plan showing locations of the different window types.

Table 2. Window and Facade Areas for Each Elevation

	EAST	SOUTH	WEST	NORTH	TOTAL
Window Area (m²)	895	1517	191	1422	4025
Wall Area (m²)	1818	3288	1818	3288	10212
Window to Wall Area	0.49	0.46	0.11	0.43	0.39

maximize natural ventilation and daylight in suitable spaces while maintaining plausible indoor lighting and acoustic effects for floors housing the auditorium and testing labs.

Middle-pivoting windows are widely used in the office levels of the IBR Building (Figure 17). This design allows users to fully open the windows when wind speed is low, and to adjust the opening when wind speed is high.

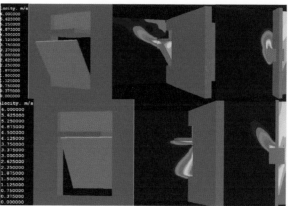

To evaluate the effect of natural ventilation using different windows, the designers used computational fluid dynamics (CFD) models to calculate how wind comes into the building (Figure 18). All the windows in the IBR Building use double-pane Low-E windows (Figure 19). This design maintains good thermal integrity for the building envelope.

from top to bottom:
Figure 17. Horizontal pivoting windows maximize natural ventilation.
Figure 18. CFD modeling of wind velocities at window openings.
Figure 19. Low-E double-pane windows are used throughout.

3.8 **Indoor Environment**

The open office design greatly enhances communication and allows workers to enjoy shared office resources. Also, this design promotes daylighting throughout the workspace.

3.9 **Lighting**

Based on the changing light levels from the outdoor environment, daylighting throughout the office spaces is integrated with controls on indoor lighting fixtures using T-5 lamps.

Figure 21 and Figure 22 show the solar tubes and skylights that provide daylight to the underground parking and basement areas.

The building uses LED lights for its outdoor lighting, primarily for the building's signage on its west and south side (Figure 23). Daylight tubes are installed in the basement garage to maximize the use of daylighting.

from top to bottom:
Figure 20. Staff floor plans are predominantly open offices.
Figure 21. Solar tubes for garage daylighting.
Figure 22. Skylights for basement areas.
top right:
Figure 23. Use of LED lights on the building facade.

3.10 **Natural Ventilation**

A displacement ventilation system is used in the auditorium in which fresh outdoor air is supplied underneath the chairs to directly cool the audience and the warmed air is then extracted at the ceiling. The exterior wall is completely operable, and functions as a "breathing" wall. This design significantly reduces the auditorium's cooling load in spring and fall. The pivoting walls can also serve as acoustic panels, and adjusting the wall openings provides a way to control of the auditorium's acoustic effects.

The auditorium is designed to use natural light, but also has controlled electric lighting for specific occasions when full control is required. Figure 25 shows the lighting system with the daylighting from the side wall.

from top to bottom:
Figure 24. Auditorium with the "breathing wall."
Figure 25. Lighting and daylighting in the auditorium.

3.11 The Sky Garden

One of the most innovative design features of the IBR Building is the sixth-floor Sky Garden, an open green space with an artificial wetland and lush vegetation planted throughout (Figure 26 through Figure 29). The space also incorporates conference areas for outdoor meetings when the weather permits. The garden floor in the IBR Building provides a relaxing space for occupants and also allows for opportunities to have meetings and discussions while closely interacting with nature. The garden floor reflects the design concept that every building or construction project actually occupies a piece of land, which belongs to the natural environment. A green building should compensate for this loss of natural environment by creating new landscaped areas within the building itself.

Figure 26. The conference area is frequently used for a variety of activities.

Figure 27. Goldfish in the reflecting pond.

Figure 28. The reflecting pond.

Figure 29. The conference area and Sky Garden.

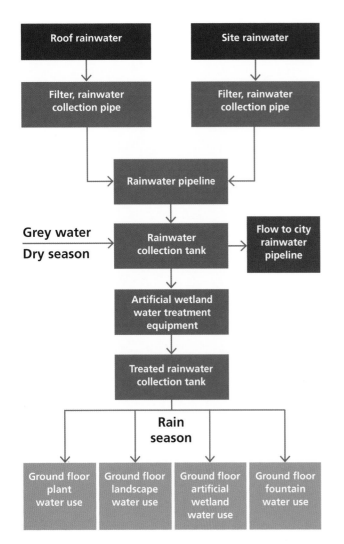

3.12 **Rainwater Collection**

The rainwater collection system is shown in Figure 30 and the flowchart, left. Rainwater is harvested from the roof and the site. Roof and site rainwater infiltrate the soil and gravel layers that filter debris, and a network of pipes collects the water. The rainwater then flows by gravity into separate rainwater storage tanks. The stored rainwater is used for landscape vegetation and outdoor fountains.

Figure 30 shows the high permeability of the paved areas and groundwater capture across the site.

Figure 31 through Figure 33 demonstrate how rainwater is used within the IBR Building and its environs. Rainwater is used in fountains and landscape vegetation. Fifty percent of the building's surrounding area is covered with green vegetation, which provides both shade and evaporative cooling.

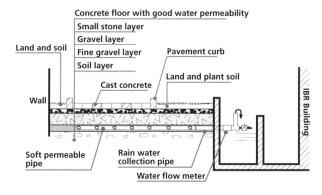

Figure 30. Rainwater recycling system.

Figure 32. Exterior landscaping with captured rainwater.

Figure 31. Groundwater capture across the site.

Figure 33. Sky Garden using captured rainwater for irrigation.

3.13 Circulation

The IBR Building's attractive circulation design, which is structured around the way people move, is meant to encourage chance meetings among the staff and invite them to use stairs rather than elevators (Figure 34). The staircase is designed with good daylight to encourage the occupants to use stairs on a daily basis to reduce elevator energy consumption. The stairs have also become a venue for competitive exercise, as staff sprint between the floors (Figure 35).

Open corridors connect the IBR Building's north and south towers. These corridors are furnished with coffee tables and sitting areas, and are decorated with green plants. It is a pleasant environment for informal breaks and a way to connect with nature outdoors (Figures 36–38).

Elevator Design

The building has two public elevators that feature variable frequency control and a power rating of 11 kW. The fire elevator also has variable frequency control and a power rating of 13.5 kW.

Figure 34. Daylit circulation between floors.

Figure 35. Daylit circulation encourages staff to exercise.

Figure 36. View of horizontal circulation at multiple levels.

Figure 37. Landscaping of horizontal circulation.

Figure 38. Circulation space between north and south towers.

Figure 39. Simulation of the noisefield at the site.

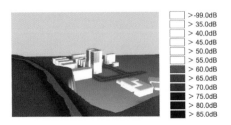

	> -99.0dB
	> 35.0dB
	> 40.0dB
	> 45.0dB
	> 50.0dB
	> 55.0dB
	> 60.0dB
	> 65.0dB
	> 70.0dB
	> 75.0dB
	> 80.0dB
	> 85.0dB

Figure 40. Simulation of the surrounding sound levels (morning).

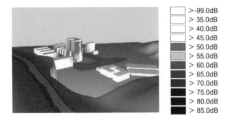

	> -99.0dB
	> 35.0dB
	> 40.0dB
	> 45.0dB
	> 50.0dB
	> 55.0dB
	> 60.0dB
	> 65.0dB
	> 70.0dB
	> 75.0dB
	> 80.0dB
	> 85.0dB

Figure 41. Simulation of the surrounding sound levels (afternoon).

Figure 42. Bathrooms have natural ventilation and daylight.

Figure 43. Urinals and toilets are flushed using captured rainwater.

3.14 Acoustic Environment

The IBR design team carefully considered the acoustic environment. Noise control is very important in green building design, because the desire to have open spaces for natural ventilation and daylighting often conflicts with the need to maintain acoustic control.

The team used computer models to understand the building's surrounding noise field (Figures 39–41). They consequently located the office spaces most sensitive to noise at the upper levels, and used acoustic control measures to isolate outdoor noise in the lower levels. The exhibition space and auditorium in the lower levels are also used less frequently than the upper office spaces, so locating them on the lower floors reduced the effects of noise on the daily activities of office staff.

3.15 Bathrooms

Because the building is naturally ventilated, the bathrooms have no air conditioning. Therefore they are located on the building's leeward side to vent odors to the outside. The bathrooms use daylighting (Figure 42), and the toilets and urinals are flushed using captured rainwater (Figure 43).

3.16 **Staff Well-Being**

The IBR Building provides spaces for the staff to exercise and to enjoy a variety of other recreational activities (Figure 44).

Ping-Pong is always popular, as are exercise machines in the fitness room. Staff are encouraged to take breaks during the day to take part in regular exercise sessions.

All the recreation rooms are daylit and decorated with indoor plants so that they are pleasant environments for a variety of activities.

Figure 44. Recreational areas for staff.

3.17 Renewable Energy

A key characteristic of the best green buildings is to have the capability to harvest renewable wind and solar energy. The IBR Building has installed a wide variety of photovoltaic (PV) systems, small wind turbines, and a solar thermal system (Figure 45). The photovoltaic system consists of rooftop PV panels, PV modules on overhangs, and a thin-film PV system on the building's west facade. The building's system was designed to generate 70,000 kWh of electricity per year (Figure 46 through Figure 47). A solar thermal system collects heat for the hot water used for the building's kitchen and guest hotel rooms.

The solar arrays are all individually metered and connected to the building's energy monitoring system, so their energy production can be analyzed (Figure 48).

Some of the PV panels are incorporated into the solar shading for the windows, so they serve dual functions in both blocking direct sun from the facade and producing electricity (Figure 49).

Figure 45. Wind turbine and PV panels on the roof.

Figure 46. Photovoltaic panels and wind turbines on the roof.

Figure 47. Photovoltaic panels on the roof.

Figure 48. Meters for the photovoltaic systems.

Figure 49. Photovoltaic panel also serving as sunshade.

3.18 Heating and Cooling Systems

The IBR Building is designed with a high-efficiency heating, ventilating, and air-conditioning (HVAC) system. Because the building is located in a hot and humid sub-tropical area, moisture control is very important for indoor thermal comfort. The building uses a temperature and humidity independent control system to treat outdoor air. A solution-based dedicated outdoor-air system is used to dehumidify outdoor air (Figure 50). This system also allows the terminal equipment to just provide the sensible cooling load of the building.

The IBR Building has different HVAC systems to accommodate different cooling needs. For example, the basement and floor use a water source heat pump (WSHP). The heat pump is located near the landscaped water pool, so the closed-loop condenser water exchanges heat directly with the landscaped water pool, which further reduces condenser water temperature while increasing WSHP system efficiency (Figure 51).

The designers included an experimental radiant cooling system for one section of the building (Figure 52).

The rest of the floors use high-performance water-supply chillers (18°C chilled water [CHW] supply temperature), with solution-based dehumidification air-handling units and fan coil units (Figure 53). Since the CHW temperature is high, the fan-coil units just manage the building's sensible heat load, a design that avoids condensing moisture and saves energy used for latent heat. Solution-based dehumidification air-handling units are used to control the indoor relative humidity. This system not only saves energy by controlling sensible and latent heat separately, it also provides a comfortable indoor temperature.

The building is designed to have relatively small air-conditioning zones. The intent was to use natural ventilation to provide a comfortable temperature whenever possible, and thereby reduce air-conditioning operating hours. For example, the balconies, hot water rooms, restrooms, and elevator rooms do not have air conditioning, relying instead solely on natural ventilation.

Figure 50. Cooling equipment located on the roof.

Figure 52. Radiant cooling as an experiment in one area of the building.

Figure 51. Fountains used to cool water in the cooling system.

Figure 53. Air-source heat pump for heating and cooling.

3.19 Hot Water System

Solar thermal collectors are installed on the building's rooftop. The collected hot water is used for the building's cafe and shower rooms (Figure 54).

3.20 Climate & Energy Monitoring

The IBR Building is equipped with instruments to collect both outdoor climate and indoor building performance data in real time. These data include outdoor air temperature, relative humidity (RH), wind speed, wind direction, solar radiation; and indoor air temperature and RH (Figures 55–57).

The IBR Building has an automatic monitoring system to measure the building's end-use energy consumption. The system also hosts the collection of energy consumption data for many of Shenzhen's commercial buildings. Energy data is collected from the building's submeters at 15-minute or hourly intervals, and transferred to the IBR's database in real time. The data from the submetering system can be used to diagnose a single building's energy performance as well as to gain better understanding about energy statistics involving the city as a whole.

3.21 Building Costs

According to the IBR, the average cost for new high-end commercial office buildings in Shenzhen in 2009 was between RMB 6,000 and 8,000 Yuan/m^2 ($88–$118 per square foot). For new middle-level commercial buildings, the average cost in Shenzhen in 2009 was between RMB 4,000 and 6,000 Yuan/m^2 ($59–$88 per square foot). In contrast, the IBR Building architects kept the total per-square-meter construction cost to RMB 4,300 Yuan/m^2($70/ft^2), which is a remarkably low number considering all of the sustainable measures included in the project. How was the IBR Building's sustainable design built on such a low-cost construction budget? By using the "design-build" model and an integrated approach, IBR saved money by managing the entire design, construction, and operation stages of the building themselves rather than outsourcing. IBR also saved money by using simple interior designs and finishes.

from top to bottom clockwise:

Figure 54. Storage tanks for the solar hot-water system.

Figure 55. Air temperature and relative humidity measured at street level.

Figure 56. Solar radiation measured on the roof.

Figure 57. Temperature and relative humidity measured at the sixth-floor Sky Garden.

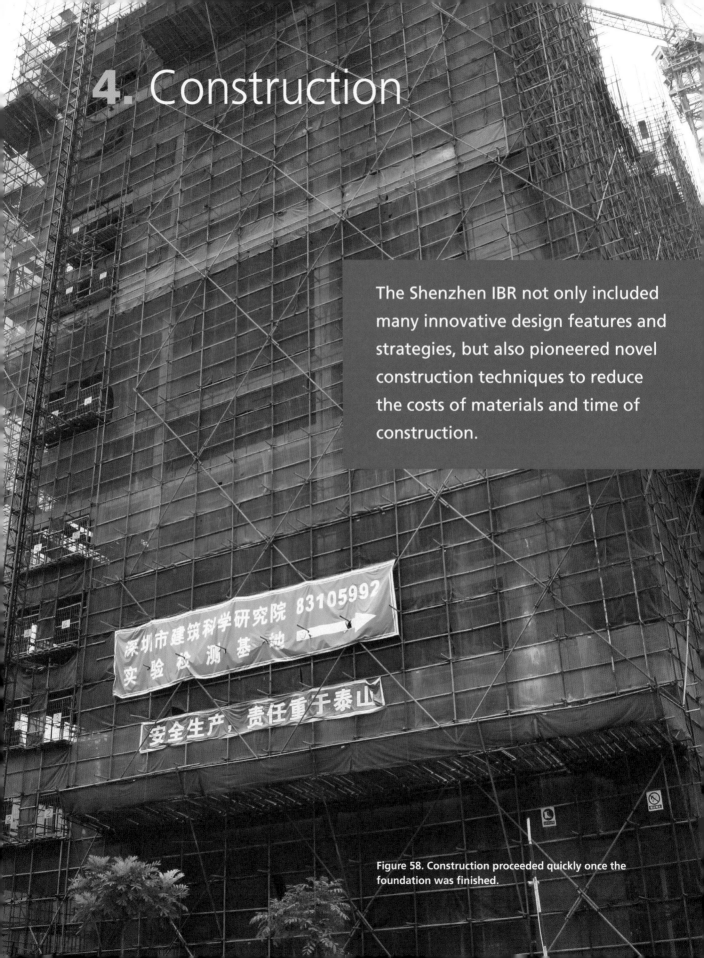

4. Construction

The Shenzhen IBR not only included many innovative design features and strategies, but also pioneered novel construction techniques to reduce the costs of materials and time of construction.

深圳市建筑科学研究院 83105992
实验检测基地

安全生产，责任重于泰山

Figure 58. Construction proceeded quickly once the foundation was finished.

4.1 Foundations

Most commercial buildings in Shenzhen use pile foundations, a design decision based on both familiarity and safety considerations. Once the foundations were completed, construction of the upper stories could proceed quickly (Figure 58). The IBR Building uses instead a raft foundation, which greatly reduces construction cost and time. The raft foundation is particularly well suited for the soil characteristics in Shenzhen. During more than 300 days of continuous monitoring, very little change in soil settlement was observed. After 1,000 days of monitoring, all soil settlement parameters met Chinese national standards. Thus, the raft foundation not only cut costs, but also met safety requirements (Figures 59-61).

from top to bottom:

Figure 59. Construction of the IBR Building's raft foundation.

Figure 60. Concrete pouring of the foundation and basement levels.

Figure 61. Construction begins on the upper floors.

4.2 Materials

Exterior Cladding

The IBR design and construction team sought to maximize the use of recycled and waste materials. One example was the use of "ASLOC board," a type of extruded cement panel (ECP) made by the Nozawa Corporation in Japan. The ASLOC-ECP is made of crushed concrete mixed with special fiber materials. Made into prefabricated panels with a high thermal insulation capability, it can be directly installed on a building's exterior walls. By replacing the complicated concrete casting process, the use of these materials greatly reduces building facade construction time.

Insulation

The building's exterior-wall insulation layer is installed using a variety of technologies (Figures 62–64). Exterior insulation LBG board, an assembly of polystyrene board and aluminum cladding, was used for the seventh floor and above. The lower levels used an environmentally friendly insulation material, partly made from agricultural waste. This interior insulation is made of a polyurethane foam board that is also comprised of agricultural raw materials such as bagasse, straw, and rice husk with isocyanate. The insulation board has thermal conductivity $\leq 0.023 W/m*K$.

Flooring

Other recycled waste materials can be found throughout the IBR Building. For example, the synthesized wood floor is made of recycled furniture, saw dust, and recycled plastic (Figure 65). The floor exhibits better durability and waterproof capability than a natural wood floor.

Carpets and Finishes

The carpets and interior finishes were selected to have low emissions and provide hard surfaces for ease of maintenance and cleaning (Figure 66).

4.3 Mechanical Systems

The mechanical systems were built in straight runs to minimize friction losses (Figure 67).

During construction, the builders discovered that the ducts were too large for the chases, and that it was necessary to lower the duct runs below the structure. In some cases, the builders had to split the ducts and reduce the depth to allow for sufficient clearance. Now the IBR uses a Building Information Model (BIM) software tool that would have recognized this problem and detected it earlier in the process.

left to right top:
Figure 62. Installing the exterior insulation layers.
Figure 63. Exterior wall insulation.
Figure 64. Sealing the thermal insulation.
left to right middle:
Figure 65. Finished wood flooring.
Figure 66. Eco-friendly carpets made with high recycled content for the "guest suite."
Figure 67. Location of building services.

4.4 **Windows & Daylighting**

The construction of the building envelope required particular attention to the detailing of the windows and curtain walls. Each orientation had a different strategy for the fixed and operable windows (Figures 68–71). In addition, a layer of photovoltaic film was installed on the west-facing facade to provide both solar electricity generation and afternoon shading (Figure 72).

this page:

Figure 68. Articulation of exterior facade showing exterior circulation, shading, and differentiation of window types by function.

opposite page, top to bottom, left to right:

Figure 69. Windows designed to promote natural ventilation at the work area. Note light shelves for deeper daylight penetration.

Figure 70. Exterior shading of south-facing windows.

Figure 71. Windows designed to promote natural ventilation and remove heat from the ceiling.

Figure 72. Photovoltaic film on the west elevation.

Figure 73. Daylit staircases to encourage greater usage between floors.

4.5 Lighting

Lighting design for the IBR Building begins with the idea of maximizing daylight, then using efficient light sources wherever daylighting is not available. The garage, corridors, and other spaces use efficient LED lighting (Figures 74–76).

4.6 Ventilation

The IBR uses several novel features for ventilation. Under-floor ventilation is used in certain areas, such as the auditorium, where it can quickly provide comfortable air-quality conditions (Figure 77).

The IBR pilot tested "personal ventilation systems," which were installed in certain cubicles and offices (Figure 78). The personal ventilation systems bring fresh air directly to the occupant's workspace without mixing with the air in the room. This approach can greatly improve the indoor air quality in the immediate ambient environment. Furthermore, personal ventilation systems only require the small amount of air required for an individual, not the air for an entire room. This design therefore can also reduce the building's heating-and-cooling energy consumption.

4.7 Special Features

The IBR Building includes several special features, including a movable wall to allow for flexible use of space (Figure 79).

left to right top:
Figure 74. LED lighting in the garage.
Figure 75. LED lighting in the meeting rooms.
Figure 76. LED lighting in the hallways.
left bottom:
Figure 77. Under-floor air diffusers.
Figure 78. Personal ventilation systems at the workstation.
right bottom:
Figure 79. Movable walls for the auditorium.

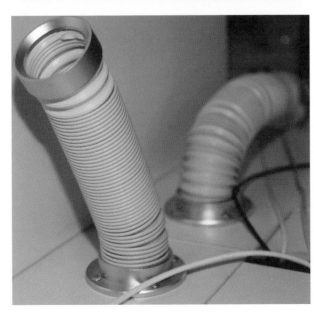

5.1 **Workplace Environment**

The workspaces in the IBR Building are designed for a variety of activities that range from individual deskwork, to collaborative teamwork, to both formal and spontaneous meetings. The design provides a wide variety of environments to support these activities (Figure 80).

Workers are encouraged to personalize their workspaces with photographs and plants. Maintenance staff check and water plants as needed (Figure 81).

Workers take advantage of the many "informal" workspaces for meetings. Figure 82 shows an example of staff meeting outdoors in the Sky Garden.

The building layout separates activities for acoustic and air-quality reasons. Figure 83 shows copy machines located in a screen enclosure outside the work areas, and ventilated directly to the outdoors to remove polluting gases (such as ozone) released when copiers are operating.

facing page:
Figure 80. Flexibility of workspaces to promote teamwork
top to bottom:
Figure 81. Workspaces with personalized greenery
Figure 82. Informal meeting space on the outside deck, in the Sky Garden.
Figure 83. Copy machines located outside the work areas and ventilated to the outdoors.

5.2 **Lighting**

The workspaces are predominantly daylit, while electric lighting is provided in areas far from the perimeter (Figure 84).

Figure 85 shows how the IBR Building utilizes daylight during the workday. The electric lighting next to the windows is turned off, while lighting is turned on in the interior area of the office space.

The target lighting levels (luminance in units of lux) for different spaces in the building are shown in Table 3.

Table 3. Target Lighting Levels (Illuminance) for Different Space

SPACE	LIGHTING LEVEL (LUX)
Design room	150
Drafting room	150
Office	100
Conference room	100
Copy room	50
Archive room	50
Corridor, staircase, and restroom	25

Figure 84. Daylit interior office space with electric lighting turned off.

Figure 85. Work spaces showing daylight control.

The actual measured lighting levels (illuminance in units of lux) for different spaces in the building are shown in Table 4.

Figure 86 shows the lighting levels in lux for the 10th-floor offices on March 26, 2010, at 10:00 a.m. The outdoor luminosity was 71,400 lux. The majority of the workspaces are between 150 and 400 lux, which is sufficient for computer-based work, and doesn't require supplemental lighting.

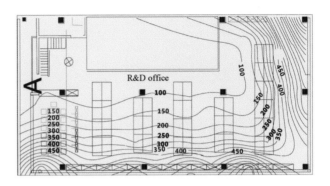

Table 4. Actual Measured Lighting Levels (Illuminance) for Different Space

SPACE	LIGHTING LEVEL (LUX)
North office mezzanine level	418
Guest apartment room	328
Employee recreation room	283
Kitchen	186
South office zone, 8th floor	185
Auditorium	173
North office zone, 11th floor	170
Lab	152
North office zone, 10th floor	124

Figure 86. Lighting levels (lux) at 10:00 a.m. on March 26, 2010, for the seventh-floor offices.

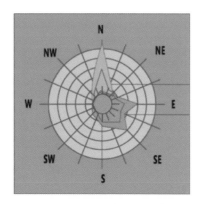

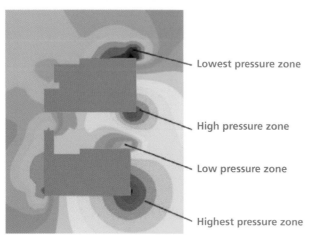

Lowest pressure zone

High pressure zone

Low pressure zone

Highest pressure zone

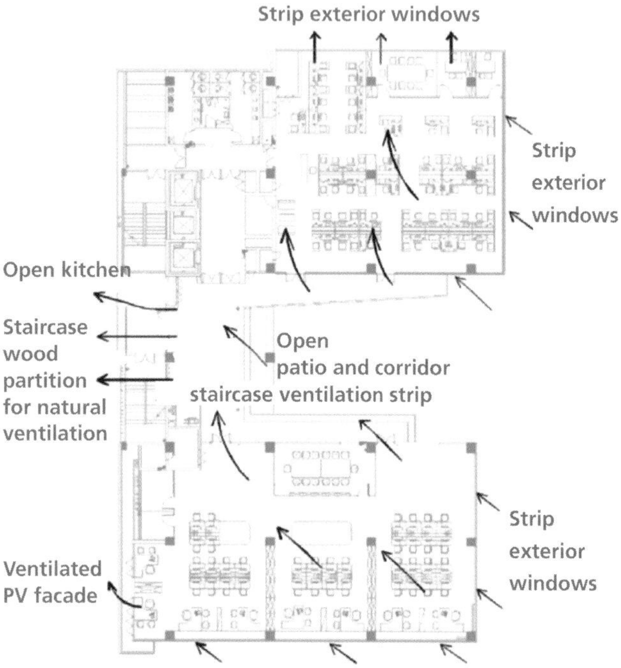

Strip exterior windows

Strip exterior windows

Open kitchen

Staircase wood partition for natural ventilation

Open patio and corridor staircase ventilation strip

Strip exterior windows

Ventilated PV facade

5.3 **Ventilation and Cooling**

The IBR Building operates for six months of the year with natural ventilation. The building was designed to take advantage of the predominant summer wind from the east (Figure 87).

The design team used computational fluid dynamics (CFD) to study how the IBR Building performed under the prevailing wind conditions. Figure 88 shows the wind-pressure field and airflow path, with the high-pressure zone on the east corners, and low-pressure zones on the west and north.

Based on these pressure zones, the airflow was designed to travel through the building's spaces as shown in Figure 89.

Figure 90 shows the ventilated cavity wall on the west side that uses both thermal buoyancy and negative air pressure from the wind to draw "stale" air out of the building.

Different window types are operated to capture and redirect the wind through the building, depending on room orientation and ventilation needs (Figure 91 and Figure 92).

top to bottom:
Figure 87. Wind rose showing wind direction in summer (red) and winter (blue).
Figure 88. CFD simulation of the wind pressure field.
Figure 89. Floor plan showing the airflow path through the building.

Much of the year, the IBR Building windows are open to promote natural ventilation. The windows are designed to direct air across the ceiling to remove the hot air without disturbing workers at their desks. In periods when natural ventilation is not sufficient to maintain comfortable conditions, the central air-conditioning system is used. Workers often use floor fans to augment the cooling through increased airflow at the workstations (Figure 93).

top to bottom:
Figure 90. Detail showing ventilated cavity on the west wall.
Figure 91. Window facing east to capture the breeze.
Figure 92. Window angled to direct the airflow to the ceiling.
Figure 93. Use of fans to augment cooling during periods when windows are closed.

Carbon-Dioxide Levels During the Air-Conditioning Season

carbon dioxide (ppm)

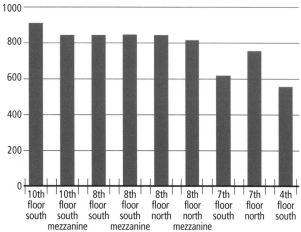

5.4 Mechanical and Natural Ventilation

The building is designed to provide mechanical ventilation for times when the natural ventilation is not available or is insufficient. Table 5 below shows the mechanical ventilation rate for different areas of the building.

Table 5. Mechanical Ventilation Rate

ROOM NAME	DESIGN OF FRESH AIR VOLUME (M³/HOUR-PERSON)
Office	40
Conference Room	21
Lecture hall	20
Laboratory	85~140
Exhibition hall	35

Table 6 below shows the natural ventilation rate for different areas of the building.

Table 6. Natural Ventilation Rate

SPACE	NATURAL VENTILATION RATE (ACH)
Office	15
Lecture hall	18
Expert's apartment	18
Basement	6~18

from top to bottom:

Figure 94. Carbon-dioxide levels during the air-conditioning season.

Figure 95. East elevation (entrance) showing the movable exterior (red) shades.

Figure 96. Exterior facade has sliding wooden shades for dynamic sun control.

Figure 97. Workspaces have mini blinds (left) and solid shades (right).

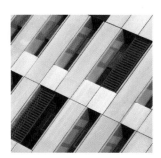

Carbon-dioxide levels during the air-conditioning season range between 600–900 parts per million (ppm) (Figure 94). During the transition season, carbon-dioxide levels drop to below 400 ppm due to the use of natural ventilation instead of air conditioning.

5.5 Shading

The IBR Building uses a combination of fixed and movable shading devices.

Movable exterior shutters are used on the east-elevation lower floors to control sunlight (Figure 95 and Figure 96).

In addition to their exterior shading, the windows have interior shading devices to allow occupants to adjust lighting levels and to control glare. Both mini-blinds and solid shades are used (Figure 97).

5.6 Landscaping

The IBR Building has a crew of dedicated landscapers to maintain the building's extensive interior landscaping. The building also includes a nursery for growing the plants that are eventually moved to the green areas. Figure 98 shows the rainwater irrigation for the roof garden.

Figures 99 and 100 show how the green areas have grown since the building opened.

from top to bottom:
Figure 98. Rainwater irrigation for the roof garden.
Figure 99. Green "rooms" located throughout the IBR Building allow workers to enjoy nature.
Figure 100. Aerial view of the green borders for the circulation.

6. A Year in the Life: Examining Building Performance

6.1 Energy Use

There are many ways to evaluate the performance of a green building over the course of a year. Does the building meet the expectations of the owner? Do the systems perform as expected? Are the energy targets being met? Are the occupants satisfied with their work environments? The IBR Building was designed to be a living laboratory. While some systems were designed to be experimental, others were designed to be dynamic, changing over time. As a work in progress, the building continues to evolve as we learn what works, and what can subsequently be applied to new projects.

Whole Building Energy Consumption

Energy use is perhaps the most straightforward performance indicator for a green building. In this report, we define the energy use as being the "operational" energy used by the building: The energy used for space conditioning, lighting, water heating, appliances, and equipment. We are not using the "total life cycle" definition, which includes the energy used in the production and transport of building materials, construction, operation, and demolition. Both definitions are used in Chinese research reports and government documents, so it is important to be clear on which definition is being used, especially when making comparisons between buildings. Also, we further define the operational energy as the "site" energy, that is, the energy measured by the meter at the site. So in the case of electricity, we are showing the energy consumed at the "site" and not at the power plant.

Table 7 shows the IBR Building's total annual whole building energy consumption. In 2011 it had a total energy consumption of 1,151,033 kWh/year, 84% of which came from the city grid. Roughly 10% of the energy used in the building was supplied by city gas mains.

Self-Generated Electricity

The IBR Building has a variety of different solar panel types, ranging from monocrystalline silicon PV modules to translucent amorphous modules, as well as a standard solar hot-water array. These different technologies were chosen to demonstrate different applications of building-integrated solar. The translucent amorphous PV was used on the west elevation to allow daylighting as well as shading. Table 8 shows the type and area for the different solar panels at the IBR.

Table 7. Annual Whole Building Energy Consumption by Fuel (2011)

ENERGY SOURCE		KWH/YEAR	PERCENT
Total Consumption		**1,151,033**	**100%**
Source	City Grid	966,567	84%
	Photovoltaic	69,555	6%
	Gas Equivalent Value	114,911	10%

Table 8. Solar Panel Types and Areas at the IBR

PANEL TYPE	MODULE TYPE	AREA (M²)
Photovoltaic	Mono-silicon PV module	136
	Poly-silicon PV module	134
	HIT PV module	125
	Translucent Amorphous PV module	600
Solar hot water	Copper and aluminum composite flat plate collector	268
	Total	**1263**

Electricity Generated at the Shenzhen IBR (2011)

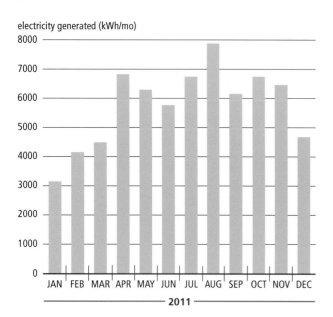

electricity generated (kWh/mo)

Electricity generated by the IBR Building's photovoltaic array was 69,555 kWh in 2011, accounting for 6% of the building's total energy use and 7% of the building's total electricity use. Figure 100 shows the monthly electricity generation at the building, ranging from a monthly low of 3,147 kWh/month in January, to a high of 7,920 kWh/month in August.

End-Use Energy Consumption

The distribution of energy use in the IBR Building on an annual basis is shown in Figure 101 and in Table 9. The largest end-use (36%) is the electricity to run the servers and other IT equipment. The next largest is air conditioning (21%) followed by "other" (18%), a category that includes laboratories, apartments, showers, the exhibition center, and elevated floors. Lighting and outlets have an annual energy end-use of 16%. Mechanical systems account for only 8% of the building's total energy use.

Table 9. Annual Energy End-Uses: Cooling, Lighting & Plug Loads, Mechanical Systems, and IT Systems

END-USE	(KWH/YR)	KWH/ M²-YR	PERCENT OF TOTAL
Air-conditioning	243,533	14	21%
Lighting and plug loads	188,127	10	17%
Mechanical systems	92,759	5	8%
Special systems (IT)	415,481	23	36%
Other	211,133	12	18%
Total	**1,151,033**	**63**	**100%**

Note: "Other" includes laboratories, apartments, showers, the exhibition center, and elevated floors.

Figure 101. Electricity generated at the Shenzhen IBR (2011).

Shenzhen IBR Building Energy End-Uses (2012)

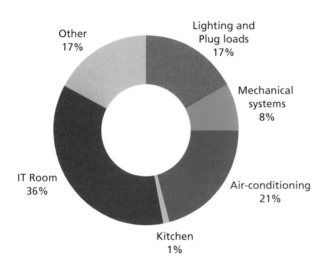

Shenzhen IBR Building Energy End-Uses (July 2012)

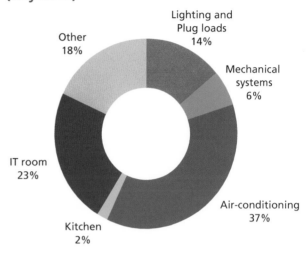

Shenzhen IBR Building Energy End-Uses (January 2012)

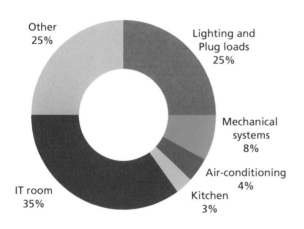

Shenzhen IBR Building Energy End-Uses (August 2012)

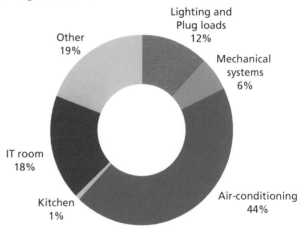

Figure 102. Annual and monthly energy end-uses.

Shenzhen IBR Building Energy End Uses (2012)

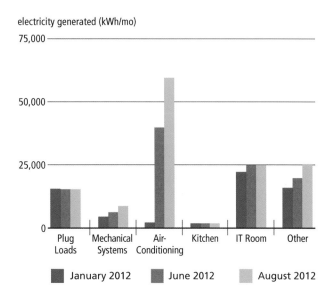

electricity generated (kWh/mo)

Figure 103. Shenzhen IBR Building energy end-uses (2012).

These end-use distributions vary by season, as very little air conditioning is needed in winter. Figure 102 on page 63 shows the energy end-use distribution in January 2012 (lower left), July 2012 (upper right), and August 2012 (lower right). Most end-uses, such as the kitchen, plug loads, and IT equipment, show little seasonal variation. Only "air conditioning," "mechanical systems," and "other" show increased usage in the summer months, with air conditioning having the most dramatic change (Figure 103).

Another way to look at the energy end-use breakdown is in the weekly profiles during different seasons. We selected a typical week's energy end-use data in three different months as shown in Figure 104. Not surprisingly, we found that in May and August, air conditioning (AC) consumes large amounts of electricity during weekdays. Typically, AC is turned on at 8:15 a.m., 15 minutes prior to the building's business hours, and turned off after 6:00 p.m. There is almost no AC energy use during non-work hours, which demonstrates that the building is operated very efficiently when it is not occupied. During the non-AC seasons e.g., in February, data center, lighting, and plug loads dominate the building's energy use.

To further understand how the building is operated, we take the peak hourly electricity use and the base electricity load and calculate the peak-to-base energy-use ratio. In May and August, the peak-base load ratio factor is 5.0 and 6.0 respectively. This is caused by the large AC electricity energy use and good AC operation management strategy. However, during non-AC seasons, the factor is only 2.6 and 2.7 because of

May Electricity Hourly End-Use

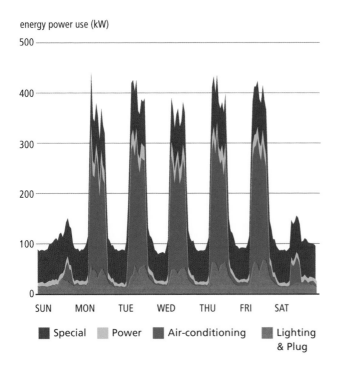

August Electricity Hourly End-Use

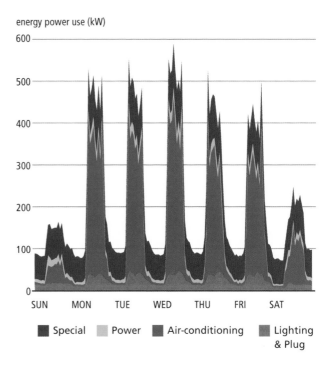

February Electricity Hourly End-Use

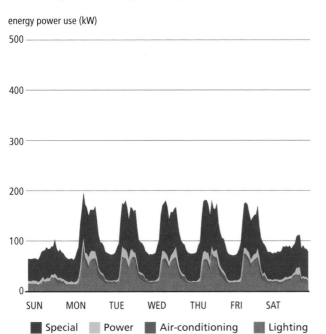

Figure 104. Typical weekly electricity end-use in different seasons.

Power Use for Plug Loads (Red) & Lights (Blue) for One Week (August 1–7, 2011) from the Eighth-Floor Offices of the IBR Building.

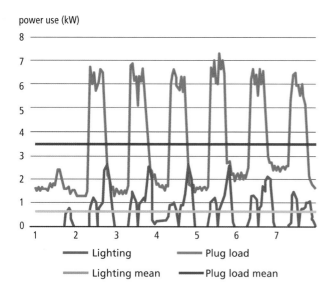

power use (kW)

Lighting
Plug load
Lighting mean
Plug load mean

Figure 105. Power use for plug loads (red) & lights (blue) for one week (August 1–7, 2011) from the eighth-floor offices of the IBR Building.

the large electricity load from the data center, which runs continuously.

Air-Conditioning Use

The IBR Building was predicted to use 33 kWh/m²-yr for air conditioning, but the actual AC energy usage in 2011 was 17 kWh/m²-yr, nearly half the predicted usage. The likely reason for this difference is that the predicted AC energy is calculated based on the Chinese commercial design standard that assumes a fully air-conditioned building. However, the IBR Building uses natural ventilation to reduce AC energy usage whenever possible, while still maintaining comfortable conditions. In a later section, we will look at the IBR Building's air-conditioning use compared to other similar office buildings in Shenzhen.

Plug Loads and Lighting

The IBR Building was designed to maximize the use of daylighting and to have lights and plug loads turned off on weekends and during periods of low occupancy. Plug load and lighting data were collected separately on a number of floors. Data from the eighth floor were selected for this analysis as being representative of the office floors. Figure 105 shows the power use for the plug loads and lighting for one week in August 2011 on the eighth-floor offices.

The mean value for lighting power during this week was 0.63 kW, with a peak value of 2.7 kW. The mean value for the plug load power during this week was 3.5 kW, with a peak value of 7.3 kW. Figure 106 shows that the lighting loads are at or near zero for these unoccupied periods. Unlike typical practice in the U.S., janitorial work at the IBR is done during the workday, so crews don't need to have lights on at night to do their work. The plug loads also show a high degree of control, in that they are mostly off at night and on weekends, but unlike lighting, there is a 1–2 kW base load value during the week.

Lighting power intensity at the IBR Building, as described in Figure 105, shows a mean value of 0.4 W/m^2 and a peak value of 1.7 W/m^2 for the lighting loads. Perhaps the best value to reflect the low lighting power intensity is the mean lighting load on weekdays, during the work period of 9:00 a.m. to 6:00 p.m., which is 0.7 W/m^2. For comparison, the Chinese standard for lighting design is 11 W/m^2 (1.1 W/ft^2), which is slightly higher than the U.S. lighting standard of 0.9 W/ft^2 in ASHRAE 90.1.[6] Clearly, the Shenzhen IBR is taking maximum advantage of available daylight during work hours, and is shutting off lights at night and Sundays.

Plug load power intensity at the IBR Building, as described in Figure 105, shows a mean value of 2.2 W/m^2 and a peak value of 4.7 W/m^2 for the plug loads. Perhaps the best value to reflect the plug load power intensity is the mean plug load on weekdays, during the work period of 9:00 a.m. to 6:00 p.m., which is 3.9 W/m^2. For comparison, the Chinese standard for plug load design is 20 W/m^2, which is higher than the U.S. plug load standard reference value of 7 W/m^2 for compliance with ASHRAE 90.1 (2010).

Comparison to Other Buildings

How does energy use at the IBR Building compare to other buildings in China and the United States? And

Power Use Intensity for Plug Loads (Red) & Lights (Blue) for One Week.

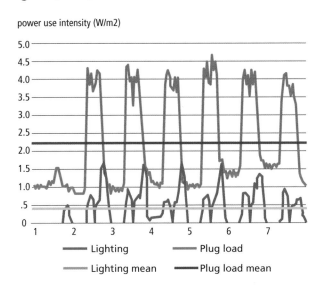

Figure 106. Power use intensity for plug loads (red) & lights (blue) for one week.

Energy Use Intensity (EUI) for 57 Shenzhen Office Buildings.

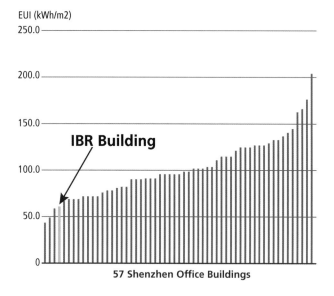

Figure 107. Energy use intensity (EUI) for 57 Shenzhen office buildings.

how does the IBR compare with other green buildings? We have a few benchmarks for comparison.

Figure 107 shows annual energy use intensities (EUI) for 57 large office buildings in the city of Shenzhen. The function, operation hours, and occupant density of these structures are similar to those of the Shenzhen IBR Building. The EUIs for these buildings range from 50–200 kWh/m²-yr. The mean value is 103 kWh/m²-yr, and the median value is 96 kWh/m²-yr. The EUI of the IBR (63 kWh/m²-yr) is one of the lowest in the sample, due in part to its use of natural ventilation and daylighting. We suspect that the three buildings in the sample with a lower EUI have only partial occupancy, or a much lower server-equipment load.

Another benchmark for comparison is the Chinese building energy data reported by the Building Energy Efficiency Research Center (BEERC) at Tsinghua University.[4] The BEERC Research Report on Annual Development of Building Energy Efficiency in China reports values of average EUIs for large (over 20,000 m²) commercial buildings in the range of 90–200 kWh/m²-yr, which is similar to the range for the Shenzhen commercial buildings shown in Figure 107.

As shown by the end-use intensities for a sample of these 57 buildings, the mean annual air-conditioning load is 36 kWh/m²-yr, with a range of 17–91 kWh/m²-yr within a sample of 14 buildings. The mean lighting and plug load value from a sample of 35 buildings is 53 kWh/m²-yr with a range of 23–82 kWh/m²-yr. Not surprisingly, the Shenzhen IBR Building values are at the low end for these end-uses.

Two references from the United States are used here for comparison with other buildings. The first reference is the U.S. Department of Energy, Energy Information Administration, which publishes the Commercial Building Energy Consumption Survey, a collection of information from a weighted statistical sample of commercial buildings.[3] The most current data are from the 2003 survey. The average energy use intensity (energy per unit of floor area) for U.S. commercial buildings from 1990–2003 was 88 kBtu/ft[2]. Compared to the U.S. reference, the Shenzhen IBR Building is remarkably low — less than 25% — of the average EUI of U.S. commercial buildings.

The second reference for comparison is a set of 22 recently studied green federal buildings in the U.S.[7] The mean energy use intensity for this group was 66 kBtu/ft[2],which was 25% lower than the average for all U.S. office buildings. But the Shenzhen IBR Building, at 20 kBtu/ft[2], is still using less than a third of the energy used by these green buildings in the United States.

6.2 Water Use

Commercial buildings use 12% of potable water in the United States. The potable water use data often includes a combination of domestic water use, landscape water use, and/or process water use.

The Shenzhen IBR uses roughly 11,000 cubic meters (3 million gallons) of water per year. Table 10 shows the split between tap water and rainwater used for irrigation and other applications.

Table 10. Annual Whole Building Water Consumption in 2011 by Source

END-USE	VOLUME (M³/YEAR)	VOLUME (GALLONS YEAR)
Tap water	6,583	1,737,912
Gray water	4,699	1,240,536
Total consumption	11,282	2,978,448

Figure 108 on page 70 shows the Shenzhen IBR Building's seasonal variation in water use, by source.

Table 11 shows the annual water consumption by end-use (domestic, landscaping, cooking, and cooling). The largest end-use is domestic water used for cleaning, showering, and drinking. Landscaping uses little city water due to the use of rainwater.

Table 11. Annual Water Consumption by End-Uses for 2011

END-USE	VOLUME (M³/YEAR)	VOLUME (GALLONS YEAR)	VOLUME GAL/ M²-YEAR
Domestic water	8,013	2,115,432	106
Landscape water	803	211,992	11
Cooking water	2,405	634,920	32
Air-conditioning replenishment	60	15,840	1
Total water consumption	11,282	2,978,448	150

How does the water consumption at the IBR Building compare to other green buildings in China and the United States? In the United State, two references are available for comparison purposes: the International Facility Management Association (IFMA) 50th percentile reference of 15 gallons/ft²-yr (150 gallons/m²-yr),[7]

Shenzhen IBR Building Monthly Water Consumption (2011)

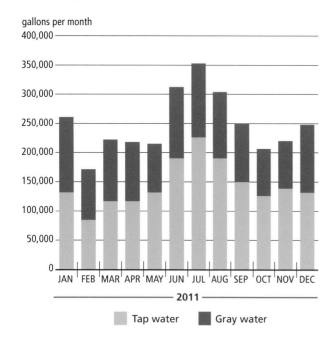

gallons per month

Figure 108. Shenzhen IBR Building monthly water consumption (2011).

and the U.S. General Services Administration 2015 target of 13 gallons/ft²-yr (130 gallons/m²-yr).[8]

6.3 Maintenance & Operations

Maintenance and operations are important aspects of energy use in high-performance buildings. One of the major reasons why buildings use more energy than predicted is that equipment is left running during periods when it is not needed. A classic example is running air conditioning or ventilation equipment when the building is not occupied.

One way to measure how well the building is operating is to plot energy use against outside temperature. Figure 108 shows a year of data for energy use as a function of outside air temperature — for weekdays, Saturdays, and Sundays. As expected, energy use is higher at low- and high-temperatures on weekdays. The energy use on Saturdays is considerable lower, and lower still on Sundays, indicating that these systems are controlled during periods of low occupancy.

The relationship between daily energy use and daily average outdoor air temperature (OAT) can be used for a greater understanding of how the IBR Building's energy performance correlates to weather data. Since the outside air temperature is not very cold in the winter, very little heating energy consumption is observed (Figure 109). In addition to sporadic electrical heating, there is a small heating system on the ninth floor. Energy use does increase with outside air temperature, but not significantly until the outside air temperature rises to 25°C. Up to that point, mechanical cooling is rarely provided, and the temperature inside the building is primarily conditioned by natural ventilation.

During the summer season (May to September), the building temperature is conditioned by the water-source heat-pump system, and electrical energy consumption increases dramatically with the increase of OAT. The peak electricity use during summer season is approximately 6,000 kWh/day, twice the consumption during the natural-ventilation season when electricity use is about 3,000 kWh/day.

6.4 **Worker Satisfaction and Behavior**

On a daily basis, the IBR has a staff of about 400 people working at its headquarters. Table 12 below shows the breakdown in staff by type. The majority of the workers are regular IBR staff (74%). Students and interns make up 7%, property management 5%, and contract staff (food service, janitorial, landscaping, security, etc.) are the remaining 14%. The average age of the staff is 32 years old.

Table 12. Occupant Data by Staff Type

TYPE	NUMBER OF PEOPLE	PERCENT
Regular IBR Staff	308	74%
Students & Interns	30	7%
Property Management Staff	21	5%
Contract Staff	60	14%
Total	419	100%

At the time of the study (2011–2012), the IBR had a staff of about 400 people working at its headquarters on a daily basis. The Shenzhen IBR Building is unusual

Building Energy Use and Outside Air Temperature

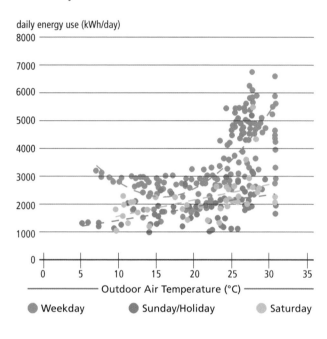

Figure 109. Building energy use and outside air temperature.

Shenzhen IBR Indoor Temperatures and Relative Humidity (2012)

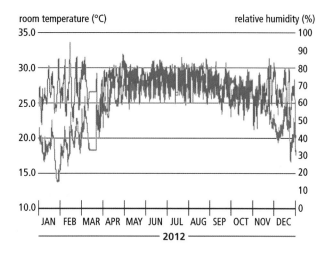

Figure 110. Shenzhen IBR indoor temperatures and relative humidity (2012).

in that it allows for natural ventilation for much of the year. Workers also augment the natural ventilation with floor fans located near the window wall.

Figure 110 shows the hourly indoor temperatures and relative humidity over a 12-month period.

The Chinese indoor comfort standard for summer air conditioning is 22–28°C (72–82°F) and 40–80% relative humidity. For winter, the standard for indoor room temperature is 16–24°C (61–75°F). The IBR exceeded these temperature ranges in 9% of total work hours, and exceeded the relative humidity ranges in 3% of total work hours.

Occupant Surveys

The IBR has conducted its own surveys, and used independent surveys as well, to evaluate the building's performance and occupants' satisfaction. Comprehensive surveys were conducted to understand participant feedback on the building's indoor-air quality, acoustics, brightness, thermal comfort, humidity level, and overall satisfaction. The building occupants were surveyed for over a year, from April 2010 through May 2011. A total of 5,908 responses from the questionnaires were analyzed. Figure 111 shows the responses to the user satisfaction survey.

Based on the survey data, we see that the majority of occupants reported satisfaction with the IBR Building's environment, with 94% expressing "satisfied" or "acceptable" overall. More than three-quarters (78%) of the occupants were satisfied with the temperature, whereas only 13% felt that the indoor temperature was too hot, and 9% felt it was too cold over the course of the year.

To further analyze the IBR Building's thermal comfort and natural-ventilation performance, we analyzed the data from the 10th floor's indoor temperature compared with the outdoor air temperature. The adaptive thermal comfort analysis is shown in Figure 112.

During 2011, the building's indoor thermal conditions met the ASHRAE 55-2010 comfort standard.[9] The majority of conditions are within 90% of the acceptability range (marked by the dashed lines), and only a few conditions lie between 80% and 90% of the acceptability limits. This agrees with the thermal comfort surveys collected for that floor shown in Figure 113, where the majority of occupants reported feeling comfortable in the naturally ventilated conditions.

Like most open-plan office buildings, the highest dissatisfaction is with the acoustic environment. While two-thirds (67%) of the staff are satisfied with the noise level in their work space, 15% find it too noisy, and a surprising 18% find it too quiet. The lighting environment has high acceptability (79%), with 15% of the staff finding it too dark, and 6% finding it too bright over the course of the year. We do not know the location of the staff responding to the questionnaires, so we cannot correlate their perceptions and their location relative to the window wall.

The indoor air quality and indoor humidity were also viewed as acceptable. Only 4% perceived the indoor air quality as "polluted," which presumably meant having a detectable odor. Most of the occupants (75%) found the indoor humidity to be comfortable, with 10% finding it too humid and 15% finding it

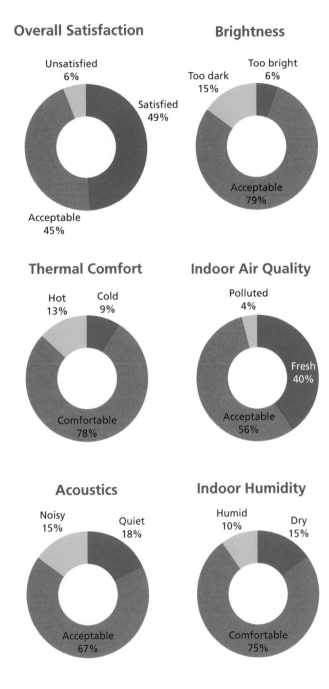

Figure 111. Responses to the occupant survey, April 2010–May 2011.

Table 13. The Test Data of Indoor Pollutant Concentration

	CO	CO$_2$	FORMALDEHYDE	TOTAL VOC (MG/M^3)	PM10 (MG/M^3)		
	(Mg/M^3)	%	(Mg/M^3)	Breathing Zone	Near the Ground	Breathing Zone	Near the Ground
China Standard limit	10	0.1	0.1	0.6	——	0.15	——
Test 1	3	0.045	0.02	0.029	0.142	0.058	0.051
Test 2	2.75	0.046	0.02	0.029	——	0.048	——
Test 3	3.25	0.045	0.02	0.029	0.142	0.067	0.051

Source: China's National Indoor Air Quality Standard GB 18883-2002[10]

too dry, over the course of the year. These findings supported the earlier surveys that reported similar levels of satisfaction, both overall and for the specific areas covered here.

Indoor Air Quality Measurements

In addition to designing for thermal comfort, the IBR Building was designed for high levels of indoor air quality (IAQ). Table 13 shows the test data of a sample of indoor pollutant concentrations within the context of the relevant Chinese standards.

Carbon Monoxide

Carbon monoxide (CO) is a colorless, odorless, and poisonous gas formed when carbon in fuels is not burned completely. It is a by-product of highway vehicle exhaust, which contributes to about 60% of all CO emissions nationwide. In cities, automobile exhaust can cause as much as 95% of all CO emissions. These emissions can result in high concentrations of CO, particularly in local areas with heavy traffic congestion. Other sources of CO emissions include industrial processes and fuel combustion in sources such as

boilers and incinerators. Despite an overall downward trend in concentrations and emissions of CO, some metropolitan areas still experience high levels.

Health and Environmental Effects of Carbon Monoxide

Carbon monoxide enters the bloodstream and reduces oxygen delivery to the body's organs and tissues. The health threat from exposure to CO is most serious for those who suffer from cardiovascular disease. Healthy individuals are also affected, but only at higher levels of exposure. Exposure to elevated CO levels is associated with visual impairment, reduced work capacity, reduced manual dexterity, poor learning ability, and difficulty in performing complex tasks. The U.S. Environmental Protection Agency's (EPA's) health-based national air quality standard (2011) for CO is 9 parts per million (ppm) measured as an eight-hour average concentration and 35 ppm as a one-hour average concentration; neither levels are to be exceeded more than once per year. (Source: http://www.epa.gov/air/criteria.html, accessed May 8, 2013.)

Particulate Matter

Particulate matter is the term for solid or liquid particles found in the air. Some particles are large or dark enough to be seen as soot or smoke. Others are so small they can be detected only with an electron microscope. Because particles originate from a variety of mobile and stationary sources (diesel trucks, woodstoves, power plants, etc.), their chemical and physical compositions vary widely. Particulate matter can be directly emitted or can be formed in the atmosphere when gaseous pollutants such as SO_2 and NOx react to form fine particles. The PM-10 standard includes particles with a diameter of 10 micrometers or less (0.0004 inches or one-seventh the width of a human hair).

Health and Environmental Effects of Particulate Matter

The U.S. EPA's health-based national air quality standard for PM-10 (2012) is 150 µg/m³ (measured as a daily concentration). Major concerns for human health from exposure to PM-10 include: effects on breathing and respiratory systems, damage to lung tissue, cancer, and premature death. The elderly, children, and people with chronic lung disease, influenza, or asthma are especially sensitive to the effects of particulate matter. Acidic PM-10 can also damage human-made materials and is a major cause of reduced visibility in many parts of the United States. (Source: http://www.epa.gov/air/criteria.html, accessed May 8, 2013.)

Meeting "Adaptive" Thermal Comfort Over the Course of a Year (2011)

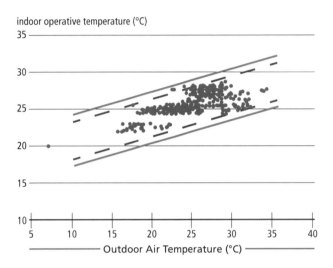

Thermal Comfort Satisfaction on the 10th Floor (2011)

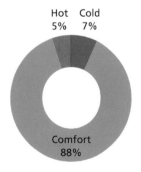

Figure 112. Meeting "adaptive" thermal comfort over the course of a year (2011).

Figure 113. Thermal comfort satisfaction on the 10th floor (2011).

6.5 **Publicity and Outreach**

The Shenzhen IBR has won numerous awards in China and internationally for its innovative design, construction, and operations. Some of the awards and honors it has won are:

1. First Grade (with highest score) of the 2010 National Green Building Renovation Award

2. First place in the National Demonstration Project of Renewable Energy Application

3. First place in the National Top 100 Green Building Demonstration Projects

4. National Educational Base for Science & Technology Dissemination

5. 2010 Shenzhen Top 10 Excellent Low Carbon Project

6. 2011 China Human Settlement Pattern Project Award

7. Innovative Practice Base for Post-Doctorate Members

8. The 3rd Biannual China Award of "Good Design is Good Business" and Best Green Design Award (by Business Week and McGraw-Hill Construction)

9. 2010 Best Practices of Building Energy Efficiency in Public Buildings by China Building Energy Efficiency Annual Report

10. 2010 Hong Kong Green Building Award, Merit Award

11. FutureArc Green Leadership Award 2011

12. The Third Biennial Top Architecture, Public Building Category, Green and Ecological Design Award

13. Futian District Practice Base for College Students, Shenzhen Municipality

7. Building the Future

7.1 Envisioning the IBR Building for Different Climates and Regions

Although the Shenzhen IBR Building was originally designed to accommodate the hot summers and warm winters of the southern China region, an IBR-inspired building could be designed for various urban or rural settings, and for different climates, in other regions of China. Figure 114 on page 78 shows how the IBR design team initially envisioned the building in different regions and climates of China.

IBR Building in Different Climates

The design for the cold climate (Figure 115) features a cube-like form, which has an efficient low surface-to-volume ratio suitable for cooler temperatures. The building has a double-glass envelope to reduce heat loss, and an interior sealed courtyard that brings the advantages of an exterior landscape to the inside of the workspace. The building was designed to operate in a high-density urban environment.

Figure 116 is a rendering of a design that would be located in a rural environment on the South China coast. The building is designed to capture the steady sea breezes, both for natural ventilation and to generate electricity. Green roofs take advantage of the area's high rainfall, and the large roof area can also accommodate PV panels. The design provides ample space for interior courtyards that allow for cross ventilation and daylighting throughout the building.

Figure 117 envisions an IBR Building located in a dry rural region in northwest China. To take advantage of the extensive solar resource, the plan calls for maximizing the roof surface for PV panels. The windows are heavily shaded by overhangs and strategic landscaping. The courtyard design allows for oasis-like outdoor spaces that are protected from the strong winds.

Figure 114. These architectural renderings show the IBR Building (left) as it was built for Shenzhen's hot summers and mild winters; (middle) as designed for an urban area in a colder climate; (upper right) as designed for a dry climate in a rural area; (lower right) and as designed for the hot coastal climate of South China.

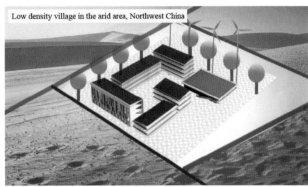

Low density village in the arid area, Northwest China

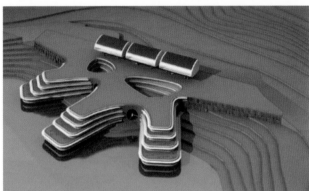

top to bottom left:

Figure 115. IBR Building in a cold climate.

Figure 116. IBR Building in a South China warm climate, located on the rural coast.

top right:

Figure 117. IBR Building in a dry rural region of northwest China.

7.2 Conclusion

The IBR Building was designed to embody green values of affordability, local materials, low-energy consumption, and transparency. The guiding principle for the design of the building was "passive design comes first, active measures come second," by which natural conditions are leveraged before adding mechanical systems to create a healthy environment. The design process started with an analysis of the climate zone and the building site conditions in order to evaluate the options for natural ventilation, natural lighting, and noise reduction. This led to an "environmental symbiosis" in which the building shape and design emerged from local environmental factors. Then, based on this optimal building shape and layout, local and low-cost technologies were selected and integrated to make natural ventilation and natural lighting possible for a healthy natural environment.

Building shape and layout design based on the climate zone and site conditions. The building shape and design were based on careful data analyses of Shenzhen's subtropical marine monsoon climate, the building site's topography, noise levels measured from the street traffic, available daylighting, air temperatures, and urban air quality.

"Concave" building shape, natural ventilation, and lighting. A concave building shape was adopted for the building based on the simulation analysis of wind and lighting conditions. The "concave" side of the building faces the prevailing summer wind from the east, while it serves to block the prevailing winter wind from the south. The width and depth of the building were developed to allow for natural ventilation and daylighting to reach all the office spaces. In addition, the level of natural ventilation during summer time was increased by slightly increasing the spacing between the two wings of the building, which increased the airflow through the plan.

 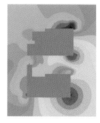 

Vertical layout, circulation, and environmental quality. Circulation for the building occupants is reflected in both the horizontal and vertical layout. The lower levels of the building were designed for facilitating human interactions and movement. Middle levels were designed for offices to take advantage of natural ventilation and daylighting, less noise, and more views, using the external natural environment to its fullest and increasing human interaction with nature.

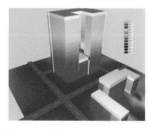

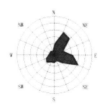 **Building layout, insulation, lighting, and air quality.** Good lighting, insulation, and air quality were made possible through the building plan, which factored in building orientation and wind direction. For example, because the east and south sides of the building

receive good natural lighting and face prevailing winds, they were designated primarily for offices. The west side of the building was designated for support space, such as elevators, stairwells, and restrooms, with restrooms and smoking areas located at the downwind northwest side. Because sunlight can affect indoor comfort, these support spaces on the west side became a natural "functional shade" for the offices.

Green elevated space, urban natural ventilation, and ecological compensation. To design a building that is in harmony with its surrounding natural environment and is accessible to the entire community, the first and sixth floors and the rooftop were built as "green" elevated spaces, maximizing the building's "ecological compensation." (Ecological

compensation is the idea that new landscaping should be introduced to make up for the loss of the natural environment when building construction

paves over land.) The open-space reception hall and the elevated man-made wetland on the first floor integrate the building and the natural environment as well as respond to the community's needs for additional green space. The elevated design not only created a garden-like environment, but also became a corridor for urban natural ventilation.

Open-space design and efficient use of space. The combination of the "concave" building shape; elevated green space; and open platforms for conferences, entertainment, and recreation has maximized the use of the building's space.

Natural ventilation. To break away from conventional fenestration design, the building uses facades that have various combinations of open windows, open walls, and ventilation grilles for optimal natural ventilation. Based on the simulation analysis of indoor-outdoor ventilation and factoring in environmental needs of the different functional spaces, appropriate fenestration was chosen in terms of window type, size, and location.

An "open facade" for interior-exterior connections. Building features, such as the open facade outside the lecture hall, the grille outside the fire stairwell, and the exterior decks, provide connections between the interior and exterior space. The exterior wall outside the lecture hall can be opened completely, and in connection with the open stairwells on the west side, creates desired ventilation by adjusting the opening angle as needed. The building uses fresh outdoor air as a source of natural cooling whenever available. This open facade element can be closed either partially or completely.

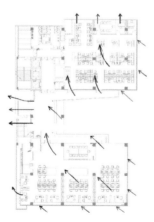

Natural lighting technology. The building's "concave" shape provided a footprint that allowed for the maximum penetration of natural lighting. In addition, the building increased natural lighting through the use of carefully designed window shapes and areas, reflective sunshades, light pipes, and the patio spaces.

Appropriate openings in the facades. For areas such as laboratories and exhibition halls that need manual control of the indoor temperature and humidity, smaller and deeper openings in the facades were used to minimize the impact of sunlight and changes in outdoor temperatures on the indoor environment, reducing the energy use of air conditioners. For office space that could take advantage of the natural conditions, bigger openings in the walls were created with bands of continuous windows to take full advantage of natural lighting.

Reflective visor and sunshade design. A reflective visor and sunshade design reflect excessive sunlight through reflector panels and light-colored ceilings to the darker areas in the interior while reducing luminance near the window areas.

Tubular daylighting system and light wells. Natural lighting was introduced to the basement through appropriate passive technologies such as a tubular daylighting system and glass light wells.

Green roofs and landscaped floors. The top floor of the building was designated for a roof garden that requires no watering system and has a solar-powered flower stand installed on top of it. The solar panels provide shade while generating power. Greening measures were used on the first floor, the middle of the building, and the rooftop to maximize ecological compensation while relieving heat from surrounding areas. In addition, each floor of the building, including the vertical shade-equipped stairwell on the middle level and the stairwells on the north side and the platform, was landscaped with climbing plants. This design provides cooling and shade.

Photoelectric curtain shading. Given the characteristic summer afternoon heat, a photoelectric curtain shade was installed on the west side and on part of the south side of the building. This technology not only generates power but also functions as a shade to reduce radiant afternoon heat, and thus increases the level of comfort in west-facing rooms. The excessive heat accumulated in the back of the curtain wall is released into the air through thermal compression in the pipe.

Design of an efficient air-conditioning system.
The air-conditioning systems were closely integrated with natural ventilation, and the indoor-outdoor temperature is monitored by the system. Natural ventilation was used as the first resort to reduce the room temperature, and the air-conditioning system would only be activated when the natural ventilation could not dissipate accumulated heat and humidity indoors.

The designers did without a conventional centralized air-conditioning system, and installed appropriately sized air conditioners for individual zones. This system provides the flexibility for the air conditioners to be used when and where needed. Due to the combination of natural ventilation and zoned air conditioning, the building uses 30% less air conditioning than nearby buildings.

Lighting system design and control. The energy-efficient lighting system was designed in terms of the type, arrangement, and control of lighting

fixtures based on the interior layout of each room, and the design and use of natural lighting. The artificial lighting system is turned on only as needed, when the natural lighting cannot meet the lighting requirements. Electric lighting is further controlled by timers and occupancy sensors.

Renewable energy. The building uses a centralized-decentralized solar hot-water system to meet the demand for hot showers by employees, and to encourage employees to use green transportation, such as bicycles to work. A solar photovoltaic (PV) system was installed on the rooftop and in the west and south facades of the building. The application of a variety of PV systems was executed for comparison studies, including PV systems composed of mono-crystalline silicon, polycrystalline silicon, HIT photovoltaic cells, and light-type amorphous silicon. PV panels were integrated with reflective visors on the south facade to both generate power and provide shading.

Water use and landscaping. An integrated system was designed to use and reuse water, rainwater, and artificial wetlands.

7.3 **Epilogue: A View to the Future Revisited**

The Shenzhen IBR Building can inspire a new green building approach that has the potential to significantly reduce harmful carbon-dioxide emissions throughout China if not the entire world. Since its debut in 2009, the award-winning IBR Building has proven to be an ideal model in sustainable building design.

Recent studies by the Energy Foundation and the China Academy of Building Research predict a turning point on greenhouse gas emissions in China's building sector around 2020 if "green building practices were implemented and building energy conservation standards were strengthened and promoted." In that scenario, by 2030 the potential for emissions reduction could equal approximately one-third of total building sector emissions.[2]

In many ways, the Shenzhen IBR Headquarters Building is a model green building. It is designed to operate in harmony with nature, resulting in lower energy use, lower costs, and high occupant satisfaction. The hope is not that this building will be replicated, but that the process and spirit that guided its design, construction, and operation can be studied, absorbed, and spread throughout the global building community.

Appendix

The IBR Building Today

Two years after the evaluation of the IBR Building, the building continues to grow. The lush vegetation planted throughout the building, in the plazas, walkways, sky gardens and elsewhere have all taken root. The extensive plantings continue to provide shade, evaporative cooling, and connections to nature for people who work there, visitors who come to learn, and the other inhabitants of the building — the birds, fish, rabbits insects, and others that inhabit this environmental showcase.

References

1. Ye, Q., *China's Commitment to a Green Agenda*, available online: http://www.mckinsey.com/insights/asia-pacific/chinas_commitment_to_a_green_agenda?cid=china-eml-alt-mip-mck-oth-1306 (accessed on June 14 , 2013).

2. Shui, B., Li, J., *Building Energy Efficiency Policies in China: Status Report*, Global Buildings Performance Network: Washington, DC, USA, 2012.

3. U.S. Energy Information Administration, *Commercial Buildings Energy Consumption Survey*, available online: http://www.eia.doe.gov/emeu/cbecs/contents.html (accessed on May 10, 2013).

4. Building Energy Efficiency Research Center (BEERC), *Research Report on Annual Development of Building Energy Efficiency in China*, 2013, Tsinghua University: Beijing, China, 2013.

5. Malone, A., *Best Green Project*, McGraw Hill Construction: New York, NY, USA, 2010.

6. American Society of Heating, Refrigeration and Air-Conditioning Engineers (ASHRAE), *Energy Standard for Buildings Except Low-Rise Residential Buildings*, Standard 90.1-2010, ASHRAE: Atlanta, GA, USA, 2010.

7. Fowler, K., Rauch, E., Henderson, J., Kora, A., *Re-Assessing Green Building Performance: A Post Occupancy Evaluation of 22 GSA Buildings*, Pacific Northwest National Laboratory: Richland, WA, USA, 2011.

8. U.S. Department of Energy, Federal Energy Management Program, *Federal Water Use Indices Website* at http://www1.eere.energy.gov/femp/program/waterefficiency_useindices.html (accessed on May 10, 2013).

9. American Society of Heating, Refrigeration and Air-Conditioning Engineers (ASHRAE), *Thermal Environmental Conditions for Human Occupancy*, Standard 55-2010, ASHRAE: Atlanta, GA, USA, 2010.

10. Ministry of Housing and Rural Development (MOHURD), *China Indoor Air Quality Standard*, GB 18883-2002, MOHURD: Beijing, China, 2002.

11. China Society for Urban Studies (CSUS), *China Green Building, 2014*, China Architecture & Building Press: Beijing, China, 2014.